LETTERS TO MY SISTERS

Pain, Poise, Pride, and God's Promise

WITH ENTRIES BY:
Paula Cotton, Mykael Dixon, Latisha Reeves Henry, Kamara Owens, Regina Roberts, Monique Ross, Valora K Starr, Taryn Wharwood, Chantell Williams

CURATED BY:
D Nicole Williams

LETTERS TO MY SISTERS:
Pain, Pride, Poise, and God's Promise

Copyright © 2020 by Sh'Shares NETWORK, LLC.

All rights reserved. No portion of this publication may be reproduced, distributed, or transmitted in any form or by any means, including photocopying, recording, or other electronic or mechanical methods, without the prior written permission of the publisher, except in the case of brief quotations embodied in critical reviews and certain other noncommercial uses permitted by copyright law.

For permission requests, write to the publisher, addressed "ATTN: Permissions" at the following:

Sh'Shares NETWORK, LLC
PO BOX 13202
Jacksonville, FL 32206-0202
http://ShShares.com

Discounts are available on bulk orders by associations and corporations for business, educational, and ministry use. For details, contact the publisher at the address above.

Library of Congress Control Number: 2020924946

ISBN: 978-1-942650-46-1 (Paperback)
ISBN: 978-1-942650-47-8 (eBook)

Printed in the United States of America
FIRST EDITION

contents

forward!..vii

introduction!..1

FROM PAIN TO PROSPERITY...3
What Is It That You Want?.. 5
You Made It... 9
beYOUtiful 11
Young, Beautiful, and Barren....................................... 15
You Really Can't Dim My Light 17
To the Woman Who Needs to Forgive 19
Dear Prospering Sister 21

CHRONIC, YET I'M HEALED! 23
Chronic Pain, But I Am Healed!.................................. 25
Dear Doubting Sister 27
What Happened.. 31
Dear Bitter, Sweet Sister 33
Doctor Sister 35

OPEN WOUNDS THAT CUT ME DEEP 37
Sunflower in Libra... 39
I Was Scared 41
I'm Angry!... 45
To the Baddest Chicks 47

FAMILY TRAGEDIES 49
In the Living Room.. 51
Should Have Loved You More.................................... 53
Dear Niece 55
One Child I Left Behind 57
Untitled 59
Missing Father 61

SITUATIONS THAT LEFT ME UNDONE 65

I Never Wanted You 67
Little Girl Lost 71
Sister of Truth 73
Sis, That Was Foul 75
Doing This Dirty Laundry 77

THINGS I NEVER SAID 81

Things I Never Said 83
The Standard 1.0 85
Dear Sacrificial Sister 87
I Wish You Would Have Told Me About You 89
Deal With It OR It Will Deal with You 93
Why Not the Good? 97
Dear Munchkin 99
September 1st 101

NO PEACE 103

White Privilege 105
Choose Life 107
Daughter of a Black Sheep 109
Menopause 111
Sister, You Hate Me 113
We Will Be Okay 117
Unspoken 121

RECLAIMING WHAT WAS LOST 123

Dear Forgiven and Free 125
Get Back Up 127
Free to Love 129
You Are Not Alone! 133
YOU 135
Baby Girl, It's Time to Listen (to Yourself) 137
The Girl Misses Her Daddy 139
Sistah Mamas: I Wonder Why 141
Black Lesbian Loves 143

MOTHERS AND THEIR CHILDREN 145

What Happened to Our Voice? 147
Understanding 149
Letter to My Mother 151

I Don't Resent You	153
The Rose of Sharon	155
Tears, for You	157

HEALING IN THE HOUSEHOLD 161
Sisters on the Run	163
Pride Over Relationship	165
I Am So Sorry, I Forgot	167
Women Who Hate Women	169

BEHOLD, I WILL DO A NEW THING (GOD-VERSATIONS) 173
Dear Determined Sister	175
Not What I Had Planned	177
When Has God Failed You?	181
No-Limits Sister	183
Is This Unto Death?	187
Hey Girl, Hey!	189
Behold My Sister	191

BLESSINGS IN THE STORM...193
Thank You After All	195
I Need You	197
Good. Girl. Friends.	199
I Call You Sister	201
Control	203
It's Almost Time!	205
Role Models	209

contributors! 211

forward

As a woman, wife, and mother of two boys, my life has gone through transformation after transformation after transformation. My life has been challenging, to say the least. I've faced depression, anxiety, self-doubt, suicide, and loneliness so complete that there were many, many days when I just wanted to close my eyes, sleep, and never wake up again. I once thought that this sleep was the only way to reach the peace I felt I needed. The reality is that as a little girl, I needed someone to hug me and tell me life would be difficult and that I would be okay. As a teenager, I needed someone to see me and understand the things I pushed through to see 16. As a young woman, I needed someone to connect to and bond with through the ups and downs of adulting. As a mother, I needed some to guide me. As a wife, I needed counsel on marriage and how to be the best wife I could be. I walked into every transition of my life basically alone. In those moments—the most critical moments of my life—I didn't have anyone I could talk to, connect with, or listen to who could make it all make sense. I didn't know what I was missing in my lack of true companionship, friendship, and sisterhood. But I made it through. Alone.

In a time when the world seems as though it is in shambles, each of us is sometimes just trying to figure out how to make it to the next minute, hour, day, or week. We could all use an encouraging word, a listening ear, and a warm hug just to be reminded that we are not alone and that someone else understands our struggles. We live through job changes, broken relationships, financial hardships, parenting issues, mental illness, and so many other situations on top of what the world throws us! Women need to know that we are not alone. *You are not alone!* Women need to understand that it is not a testament to our true strength when we endure things alone. Yes, maybe you can handle it;

maybe you are tough. And I know many of you have always handled everything on your own, just as I have, but you don't need to.

Most of us women simply do not know how to ask for help. We don't know how to receive support. Some of us don't know how to maintain bonds with other sisters. We don't understand how important sisterhood is on the road to finding true purpose. When we connect with women to help ourselves, we develop an openness that allows us to achieve personal goals while building our sisters up at the same time. Because I've not always been able to develop through one-on-one, in-person conversations with women, books that give me wisdom build me up to eventually build connections with my sisters.

Every book from Coach D Nicole has stretched my spirit further than I knew it could stretch. The most impactful thing I have learned from Coach D is that our purpose in life has already been predetermined. On this journey called life, we will go through some things that we do not understand at that moment, and we might not understand them many moons later either. Eventually, we learn that obstacles are placed in our lives to prepare us for that preordained purpose. We then become more willing to do the work that is required

As you read through these letters, I hope you see that you are not alone on your journey. I pray you see yourself in the stories of your sisters. Through hearing their pain and triumphs, I pray you learn to face your own so you can move beyond what hinders you from being most authentic. In reaching for your purpose, my hope is that you are inspired to move past old pains so you can truly live.

My friend and sister, D Nicole Williams, and all the sisters who contributed to this book share the most intimate parts of themselves on these pages. I hope reading this book inspires each of us to share as well. And as we share more freely, we learn to be there for our sisters as they work to share their intimate parts too. This book demonstrates that, as women, we share many of the same or similar experiences. I hope that as you read, you can reflect and grow with your sisters through their pain and redemption and allow their words to help you grow through your own experiences.

—*Erica Robinson*

introduction

Since I was a young girl, I always hoped to understand women better. As a young woman now living through the middle ages of life, this desire has only grown more pronounced over time.

In my youth, I watched my mother live through things that I did not understand back then. I watched my mother grow through diverse challenges that even the women around her were not experiencing at that time. Now, as an adult, I am still shocked to hear the extent of her life's story—trinkets of which I only come across in settings when she ministers to communities of women by sharing her deepest troubles. My mother is not an open woman, yet as she ages—and as I age—I'm discovering how beautiful it is to create intimacy by listening to her story, by listening to her share as only a woman can.

Good mothers groom daughters to further their legacy and live the best lives possible, yet mothers do not always share their personal stories of womanhood. In fact, one of the greatest strengths of womanhood overall may reside in a woman's ability to protect young daughters from the pains of being a woman. In this calculated abyss of silence, which is a testament to our resilience and strength, we remove an essential component of a young woman's grooming by preserving secrets. And as a black woman, I am well-acquainted with the pattern of blackness that keeps quiet on matters which other folk might not understand. Assuming that other women don't understand us is a faulty judgment that keeps us separated from one another, and from ourselves, simply because we do not voice misfortunes. If we assume that too much sharing only hurts us, we do not share in ways that will help us.

All too often, women pass one another as if we're living different lives in different spaces. However, wisdom taught me at a young age that we largely live the same lives in different bodies. We suffer through insecurity, depression, and being overlooked and misunderstood. Whether women share identical experiences or not, we basically want to be loved, included, supported, and groomed to live our best lives. Sharing gender in a world that treats so many of us the same means our experiences align even when our social context does not. Whether rich or poor, black or white, African or Asian, women share a connection that transcends demographics. The day we come to appreciate this value will be a day when we can all behold the beauty of truly being sisters.

With *Letters to My Sisters: Pain, Poise, Pride, and God's Promise,* our intent is that this grand release encourages all our sisters to share and release as well. To reveal censored areas of womanhood, black female authors of diverse backgrounds confronted their deepest pains to release burdens they have held for far too long. With these letters, we commit to saying what we mean to say and healing in formally forbidden areas of life. No longer will we keep our herstory private. As we share with one another increasingly, we create a pattern that rewrites a tragic history of silence.

Because this book sheds light on incidents that women have been silent about for a lifetime, my deepest prayer is that the words of these pages create a foundation for us to embrace womanhood in new ways. These letters have been written from the heart. As such, they are meant to prick us in ways that draw us to one another as we draw closer to self. The mind-body-soul alignment offered within this book serves women by disclosing the hidden tragedies and triumphs of womanhood. Though we may never share the depths of our souls with the sisters who impacted us directly, it has been our greatest joy to release these heartfelt connections so women all over the world can embrace their own impacts and begin living more fully.

As you read, I encourage you to also write. Don't miss this opportunity to share your own letters. If you're up to it, send those letters to the sisters who deserve to hear your heart.

God bless you.

—D Nicole Williams

From Pain to Prosperity

What Is It That You Want

To the Woman Who Is Afraid to Choose Herself,

"What is it that you want?"

On the verge of heartbreak, one of my close friends asked me that poignant question, and I couldn't answer. There was so much I could and wanted to say, but I was silent. It was a silence that never came when someone asked me to fix their problem, do something for them, or even when they asked for advice. Here I was with someone who asked *me* what *I* wanted, and…

I had no answer.

At that specific moment, they were asking me what I wanted from my relationship. What were the top three things that I needed? I fumbled some answers out, saying the three most important things to me are time, honesty, and support—not financial, but just that extra boost of assurance when life throws me a curveball. When I listed off those three, my friend proceeded to ask me if I was getting all three of those things; I said no. They asked if I was getting two of the three; I said no. They asked if I was getting one of the three; again, I said no. To these denials, they responded, "If you're not getting any of those, and they are most important to you, why are you staying?"

I couldn't answer with anything more than tears. I was staying because of the time I'd put in. I was staying because I'd cried too many tears, prayed too many prayers, and I'd given too much to just up and leave. That's what I thought. By not being able to give a clear reason that I was staying in an unfulfilling relationship, I realized that what I had begun to value as success in my relationship had caused me to lose a sense of self. I wasn't receiving anything that I wanted. Still, somewhere in me, I thought staying and making my relationship work meant I was successful. Until I answered that question, I never realized that staying meant I was agreeing to never have what was important to me. That wasn't the life I wanted to live. That's not the life for anyone to live.

The only thing left to do was to make a decision. I had made it to a place in life where I thought I was successful, yet my victories in the current stage of my life were wrapped up in the success of others. That may sound bad, but it's not. I'm the one people turn to in their tough moments. They come to me, pour their heart out, and wait on my response. My words hold weight with them, so I choose words carefully. I check in on people and make sure they make it through tough moments. When people end up feeling better, I feel better. I had been that way so long that until I was asked what I truly wanted and found myself struggling to answer, I didn't realize that I had forgotten about myself. I was struggling to identify with what my heart wanted and what it was that brought me joy. I was struggling to know who I was when I had nobody else to support.

Losing yourself in your work and life is not the end of the road, but when it happens, you must be willing to do the work to get back to the core of who you are. You can't be defined as just a daughter, just a mom, just a sister, just a wife, or whatever your role is as a woman. You must make sure you know who you truly are aside from those titles. You have to know what makes you smile.

With this conversation, I took a step away to just exist outside of my relationships with people. I took the time to find who I was outside of everything I had going on. I went places alone and rediscovered things about me that had been obscured by daily life. I put in the self-work and realized that settling for a relationship that wasn't giving me what I wanted just wasn't worth it.

If you can relate, you are not the first woman to be here. Each day comes, and we have tasks to complete. What doesn't get done in one day just rolls over to the next. We get caught up in getting things done, and sometimes, depending on the magnitude of the things we need to get done, we simply push ourselves to the back burner over and over again. Trust me: I know how you feel! Now, you're just fighting to find time for yourself because you've lost sight of what it is that you truly want. Sometimes we are afraid to let go of where we are because the life we created used to be so amazing, but you deserve better. *We* deserve better.

Take the necessary time to find what brings you joy, and don't be afraid to let go of what it is that doesn't. Every day won't be perfect, but every day shouldn't be miserable either. Walking away is hard, but sometimes, it's the best thing you can do. You'll look back one day and wonder how you stayed unfulfilled for so long. I've been there where you are, but trust me when I say… life is much better when you finally find the answer to the question: What is it that you truly want?

—Finally Here, Finally Free

You Made It

Mama,

I'm so proud of you—you have been doing amazing lately. Do you remember all those times you were just barely making it—the times you didn't have enough money to buy anything extra? It used to break your heart to hear your baby ask for small things in the checkout line when you couldn't buy them. Now, you're buying things that go well beyond your baby's dreams, and you're not struggling to do it!

I remember you struggling all those nights with ideas, not knowing if they were good or not. You stepped out and took a chance; now, look at you. You are amazing. You are thriving. You are doing just fine.

It doesn't matter anymore who doubted you. It doesn't matter anymore who never came to help. The people who always said they were going to do something to help you never did it, but guess what? You survived. You are stronger now. You have stared adversity in the face and tackled every situation headfirst.

Nothing about your life gave you the upper hand. You did not always make the best choices. Often, the choices you made put you directly onto the path toward another letdown or heartbreak. But every time life knocked on your door, you answered with poise and grace. Look where it got you. Look where it's going to keep taking you.

Keep going, Mama. God has your back!

You are not the little girl that people used to look over anymore. You are not the vulnerable teenager that they took advantage of. You are not some restless woman that they tried to label bitter and scorned. You are a fighter. You are an overcomer. You are a warrior! You are an accomplished lady, and this is just the beginning. You've been stepping out and taking chances and think about how that confidence has been paying off.

Now, let's be transparent; there are still some things you've been holding back on. You still have some ideas that you are scared to take the first step on, and that's okay. Just take this time to appreciate where you are and be proud of where you are. Stop looking at how far you have to go and take time to look at where you are going. Your final destination is forever moving. Your goals are growing, and once you attain a goal, it's time to move the mark, so stop looking at what's left and take a moment to look at what's done. Congratulate the woman who made that possible!

Mama,

They told you that they didn't expect you to amount to much. They were wrong! They told you that you would only be good enough for second place. You are first! They told you that you would have to figure it out on your own, and you did!

I had to stop and tell you how proud of you I was because some people didn't make it this far. Some people made it here only to turn around and go back. You stayed in the fight. Some days are harder than others, but you are still here. By the grace of God, you will always keep moving forward.

Be proud of YOURSELF.
I already am.

—Your Biggest Fan

beYOUtiful

GIRL, GIRL, GIRL!

This is a long-overdue conversation.

I feel like you have many reflective moments, but it's time to put it ALL out there. Get it off ya chest! Now is the time for you to stop blocking stuff out and leave it all on the table. When you are trying to grow, you cannot take any of that old mess with you, okay?

Okay.

Honestly… honestly, I am SUPER proud of you and the woman you are becoming. You have come a long way, especially mentally. You always wanted to blame your past toxic relationship for why you were overloaded with self-doubt, insecurities, and suicidal ideation. But it was the people you were surrounded by when you left your mom: the family members who were supposed to create a home for you and not just a space to live in. It was your cousin who poured hate into you. After your mom stopped raising you and your father got locked up during your childhood, the thing that really tore you down was your cousin. Your cousin!

How could you ever allow her to have that much power over you? Most people would be devasted by not having their parents in their lives, but you—you stood strong. All it took was for this one lady to talk down to you, and it broke you.

I am glad you finally realized where your mental distress originated from. It was never your fault. It was just time to BOSS up and learn from the pain. But the lack of love growing up did lead you down a path full of trouble. You made decisions out of hurt, looking for attention and love: the love that you didn't receive growing up.

But now we've got that out the way, you should have recognized the signs before getting with him. Yes, we are going to get down to the bottom of it as much as we can. I don't know what it was about him or what it was about you at the time, but it was like you completely let yourself go. You had no sense of logic. What did you see in him? You were really stuck on the fact that he knew how to dress? He was a poet. He could dance. But is any of that useful in helping you grow?

The minute details lured you in, and BOOM, you were stuck. You did things because it felt good to the flesh. You allowed yourself to entirely fall into this long, winding trap. He was younger than you. You thought he was mature enough to be with you, but you did not know him at all. You really didn't learn who he was until years later.

You allowed this boy to toy with your heart multiple times and with various women that you knew. Not ONCE did you decide that enough was enough. God was probably showing you lesson after lesson the entire time, but you chose to believe what you wanted to. Spirit of discernment, where? You were already broken yet, you continued to play yourself.

You poured so much of yourself into him and couldn't save even a little bit for you. You allowed him to run your financial accounts dry. You allowed him to put you in deep debt. You allowed him to break you down further than your cousin ever could. You were at the end of the road, trying to make things work with him. You were ready to commit suicide, but glory to GOD, you found an ounce of sanity. You pulled yourself together and cut off that dead weight. Even though you considered getting back with him, God said enough is enough. You showed up to the fight, and God fought the battle for you, and that boy left running.

The devil could no longer trap you in what seemed to be a never-ending cycle. It was time to regain all your strength and confidence. It was time to achieve everything you could dream of: financial literacy, wealth, success, and overall happiness. You did just that!

But why is it that sometimes the thoughts creep up on you? "What happened?" "What did I do wrong to make him leave?" "What if?" NO!

The enemy will tempt you! The enemy will use what used to damage you to try to make you relapse. But when you are filled with Christ's love, all of that is just on the surface and can be knocked off.

It is time to live the life you deserve.

You have overcome so much.

You are stronger mentally. You are no longer depressed. You are no longer suicidal.

You are *beautiful*.

You are *loved*.

You are *strong*.

You are *confident*.

You are everything you are supposed to be:

beYOUtiful.

—*Be YOU*

Young, Beautiful, and Barren

Dear Young, Beautiful, and Barren...

"Lord, I didn't mean what I said!"

I was just a young girl. I didn't know any better. The many years of saying I NEVER wanted to have kids... Little did I know that I was speaking my state.

Growing up as a little girl, I never wanted to have kids! But to be STRUCK with an ailment at an early age that resulted in a life-altering state is just disappointing.

Doesn't barren mean broken?

I repeatedly asked, "Why?"

Lord, I know you created me for a purpose. I know that you alone know the plans you have for me—to bring about a future of prosperity and not a disaster. But this feels like a disaster!

Where is the prosperity in this? This isn't what I hoped for. I mean, I didn't necessarily want kids, but I didn't want the ability taken away from me either.

No more baby showers, baby dedications, or anything for me! How can I celebrate others expecting a child when I'm a young, beautiful, and barren woman? How am I supposed to enjoy my marriage without the ability to give birth to our children? I am grateful for a loving and understanding husband who loves me unconditionally and embraces my barrenness. Still, I just wish it could be reversed. At least, the ability would be there, and we could attempt if we desired to.

God, are you mad at me?

If you aren't mad, I am just living out the harvest of my own sown words. Life and death are in the power of the tongue, and it looks like I sowed the seeds for my barrenness—the pain, the pressure, and the pursuit of answers.

Lord, I need a revelation; I need peace about the positioning of my wound. No longer am I consumed with WHY, but I want to know what? What am I to do with a barren womb? Can I be fruitful and multiply in this journey without giving natural birth to children?

Barren doesn't mean broken!

This revelation chilled my soul, calmed my anxieties, clarified my purpose, and cleared me from shame while ushering me into freedom! Oh, my goodness—why has it taken me so long to embrace barrenness as a blessing, not a burden? Wrestling with whether I was cursed or just chosen was overwhelming.

I wish someone had told me when I was younger, "Don't say that!" I didn't realize my words could take root. However, I realize now that though my words have life and death in them, I was created for a purpose far bigger than my pain.

I am FREE today because though my womb is infertile, my life is fruitful. I've embraced my barrenness as a part of my journey. I am turning fruitfulness into faith by producing the most significant outcomes of my life, all to the Glory of God! God has chosen me, and for that, I am grateful! Ministry has become my mothering. Truthfully, I am honored to be a vessel of spiritual births!

—Barren, but not Broken

You Really Can't Dim My Light

DEAR SIS,

Let me tell you something…

I love you, but I really don't like you. I know you didn't expect to hear this, but it's been on my chest for a while; I just never knew how to say it. Maybe it's because you tried to put the fear of you in me, and I listened. Or perhaps it's because you repeatedly tore me down with your words. The combinations of these things caused me a lot of pain, self-doubt, and insecurity over the years. I don't think you know that being raised by you affected me in the worst way.

Now, again, I'm not saying you don't love me, but you had a complicated way of showing me your love. My mother may not have been stable enough to take care of me, and my father may have been locked up, but that was N E V E R the time for you to experiment with being a "mom." You saw the opportunity to take in a "lost child," and you took advantage of the circumstances.

You were like Miss Hannigan in the movie *Annie*. You were the reason my whole life has been centered around money as opposed to love. Why did you keep tallies on everything you did for me as if nothing you did was out of love? YOU decided you wanted to take me in! You held your care over my head, so when I became an adult, it was like I owed you for raising me.

At this point, I'm forever grateful for not being stuck in the situation I was in but know this: I shouldn't have been mistreated for it. It's not my fault my mother and father made the decisions they made.

And that's another thing...

I LOVE my parents, regardless of their mistakes and their choices. God gave me a forgiving heart, and I NEVER held a grudge or carried a burden because my parents didn't raise me, but it seemed like YOU wanted me to. You always had something negative to say about my mom, and you wanted me to lack hope that my father would get out of jail.

Who does that?!

You may pretend like you don't remember these things, but trust me, these are things that I will never forget. I can't, but I want you to know that I have outgrown you. I know you are insecure and uncomfortable with yourself. Still, nothing justifies you deciding to hit me for no reason, smack me for no reason, and slander my parents for no reason.

As I have gotten older, I've started to self-reflect. I realize that just because someone puts a roof over my head and feeds me doesn't mean I have to pay for it by accepting disrespect. Instead of retaliating to the poor treatment, I prayed for you. I honestly wanted nothing from you but a sister. I wanted nothing but someone I could trust and talk to whenever I had issues. The thing is, I never felt comfortable talking to you about anything. The house was just a house—it was never a home, so I had to get out the first chance I could.

Even as you watched me grow and become a better person, you allowed your demons to really control you. You accused me of stealing money as I tried to get out and decided to change the locks, so I felt unwelcomed there: at the house that was not a home.

I know I was never welcome.

That's okay though. All that you thought would push me down only made me rise higher. You should understand that there is literally nothing you can do to make me stoop down to your level. I'm out, and I've been blessed to have my own. I've got my strength back and am really making moves out here.

I guess I should thank you for the drama because I wouldn't be the force I am today without that childhood experience.

Dear Sis,

YOU can't dim my light!
NOTHING can dim my light.

—The Sister Who Built a Home from Your Empty House

To the Woman Who Needs to Forgive

Trigger Warning:
Be Advised That This Entry Will be Triggering for Readers

TO THE WOMAN WHO NEEDS TO FORGIVE:

After all this time, I am finally ready to forgive him. I never thought the day would come that I would be free from that night on that cold tile with him on top of me. He has been a weight around my neck for over fourteen years, the worst form of hidden secrets and overt scars.

I was thirteen. I had never had sex before in my life, never been kissed; I barely held hands. I still thought the ultimate life goal was to be like the princesses on TV. What he took from me went far beyond that moment. He made me a victim, and the world made me a criminal. No woman should ever be blamed for her rape, especially not a little girl.

That moment opened my life to a world where whispers spoke louder than screams. I had nightmares of him. For months, I could not sleep. I had nightmares of that floor and the light that seeped under that bathroom door. I heard the music and prayed to see the footsteps of someone walking in to save me. No one ever came, and instead of someone saying that they may have failed me in that moment, all they could say was: I asked for it.

Instead of saying I would get over it, they should have asked me if I was okay. Instead of saying I asked for it, they should have heard me scream, "NO!" While they were blaming me, they should have held him accountable, but instead, they picked up his hung down head from shame as if he had fallen victim to some sort of entrapment.

They kept him in prayer and kept me in bondage.

I hated him for that; what he did made me hate myself. The fact that anyone could see me and find me beautiful after he had laid me to tile as a mop bothered me. I felt drowned in his actions, tainted by his touch. In rooms where I should have been safe, memories of him were a loaded gun.

What happened was not okay, and now I know it was not my fault. I forgive him. It took years of wanting to cause those same scars to his character that he physically caused me. I wanted the world to see what he had done to me. It took years to move past wanting the world to realize that I did not rape myself.

I let hate and fear hold me so long that it ate away at my potential until one day when I realized it was time for me to let that pain go. Where I once wished him pain, I now wish him peace. Where I wanted him to hurt, I now hope he is healed. It feels crazy to say, but not forgiving him has been a poison to every relationship in my life.

My Dearest, Sweet Sister,

I understand how comfortable your pain has gotten. You have sat in it and allowed it to change who you are. You have allowed it to eat away at you. I allowed it to eat away at me, but when I was ready to be free from the pain, I started by freeing him of my rage. I no longer wanted to be broken with him because broken pieces cause scars.

Sister, it is time to heal your wounds, free yourself.

—Forgiving and Free

Dear Prospering Sister

DEAR PROSPERING SISTER,

Pain is inevitable, and prosperity is attainable. This is something that I have embraced on my journey from pain to prosperity. Many times, we encounter roadblocks along the way that are not just painful; they are crippling.

When I looked at the word crippled, I saw myself: severely damaged and malfunctioning. Oh, my goodness! That was me! For a moment, I felt that I had been crippled in my pain, and prosperity was out of reach. Even while I began to embrace that prosperity is attainable in my pain, I just couldn't seem to grasp the concept of being courageous and crippled. It just made sense to my human, natural mind to get well before attempting to be prosperous.

My Bible says, "Beloved, I pray that you may prosper in all things and be healthy, even as your soul prospers" (*3 John 1:2 WEB*). So, in essence, it made sense for me to heal first. Besides, I was in a whole quandary with the Word because I was questioning the state of my soul! Even though I knew that my soul was prospering, this body felt like it was on a different level. I had to wrestle with the idea of prospering in pain and from pain.

Having this mindset has always ushered me into a greater appreciation for my pain because it ultimately birthed purpose that became my pathway to prosperity. Everything I have ever experienced that was painful has been used by God to produce something greater out of my life.

Prosperity hasn't always been money. The people, places, and experiences I have been exposed to from my pain have been as profitable as the income-producing opportunities I have had due to my pain. These opportunities taught me to embrace my pain and the crippled nature it produced in me. Opportunity forced me to see my condition as a means to wake up my courage. I was forced to stop seeing myself as damaged goods.

Though I may be damaged physically, I am still a good package.

God has done so much with my pain. How dare I complain about the blessings I've received from it? While it is a physical burden, it's a spiritual blessing. I realize that pain may very well be the vehicle to my greatest victory.

I AM BLESSED.
My pain has led to my prosperity.

—From Pain to Prosperity

Chronic, Yet I'm Healed!

Chronic Pain, But I Am Healed

JUST HEAR ME OUT SISTERS…

"Pain, pain go away.
DON'T come back another day."

This is my daily rant as I journey through my physical process. As much as this chronic pain can be agonizing, annoying, and aggravating, I have discovered that it's a privilege and an affirmation of my faith to carry this cross. I've embraced that healing is necessary to fix what's broken. Wholeness means fixing things so they are aligned and so that all things function effectively. Even in my pain, it's a process.

Healing, for me, is a declaration because I know Christ died for my healing. It's the daily journeying with pain that I must come to grips with while also having the grit to keep pressing forward.

There are so many days where I feel so weak but still committed to winning! Winning is an attitude; it's not an emotion. If winning were based on how I felt, I would lose most days, but winning, for me, is a daily declaration as I pray through this journey.

The moment I knew my condition would be long term, it was a blow to my whole being. Aside from the debilitating physical pain, the emotional toll was most intense. I can still recall the defeat and helplessness I felt; I can still hear the questions I asked. "How will I be productive?" "How will I effectively be a wife?" "What about all those things I have committed to that require my presence, persistence, and productivity? Lord, this can't be what my life will look like? I'm crippled from an injury, and the result is chronic pain? My goodness! The recovery from the injury is difficult enough. Still, now I have to continue recovering while finding the right blend of meds, therapy, natural products, and medical equipment to manage this condition. It took much prayer, support, counsel, and seeking ways to undergird my mind, thoughts, and attitude to live like I'm healed while hurting. I wish I could put into words the intensity of my daily pain, such as the challenge of sleeping at night or the adjustments needed in my home to simply live. But I am healed; I just have to keep believing it.

I'm healed because I can endure and produce. I'm healed because I am still breathing. I'm healed because I've decided that NO MATTER what I face or encounter physically, I press on!

There is a Blessing in Pressing.

My constant reminder to myself is, "Girl, you got this! Keep pressing, keep believing, keep trusting, and keep smiling!"

As much as I feel charged with this physical thorn, I am duly qualified for healing.

—Pressed and Still Blessed

Dear Doubting Sister

DEAR DOUBTING SISTER,

"Don't stop believing!"

This is what I say to myself every day. I look in the mirror and say it daily. The word *believe* means having certainty in the reality, actuality, or trustworthiness of something. To believe is to have assurance in the sincerity of positive claims. It means to give credence or to place one's trust in God's truth. A believer is one who takes God at His word and trusts in Him.

Several years ago, I suffered a severe spinal injury. As a young, married, vibrant woman, pursuing the will and purpose of God, I thought, "Lord, what is going on?" I was serving the Lord, serving in the ministry, and had recently changed careers. I was doing good! My relationship with God was solid enough for me not to crumble. But what I discovered was my encounters with Him were about to evolve.

I went into a spinal surgery walking but came out with walking complications. I went in expecting one outcome and came out needing an expected end that only God could bring about. When I went in, there were some things that I was accustomed to relying on, but I came out with complete reliance on one source—that source was God.

I feel that every believer has been given a mandate as a disciple to Believe GOD! It is very clear to every believer of the Word of God that, without faith, it's impossible to please God. To believe, one must have faith! You talk about going from saying it in the mirror to saying it to move—that was ME!

I spent time searching the Word and getting an understanding of faith. The term *faith* is defined as a belief in or confident attitude toward God, involving a commitment to His will for one's life. Searching the Word, I found faith in scripture:

> *"For the gospel reveals how God puts people right with himself: it is through faith from beginning to end. As the scripture says, "The person who is put right with God through faith shall live."*
>
> ROMANS 1:17 GNT

> *"Clearly no one who relies on the law is justified before God, because "the righteous will live by faith."*
>
> GALATIANS 3:11 NIV

> *"But my righteous one will live by faith. And I take no pleasure in the one who shrinks back."*
>
> HEBREWS 10:38 NIV

> *"But when you ask, you must believe and not doubt, because the one who doubts is like a wave of the sea, blown and tossed by the wind."*
>
> JAMES 1:6 NIV

I was encouraged because I realized that believing GOD is possible and believing GOD is beneficial. Thank you, Lord.

DEAR DOUBTING SISTER,

It has been refreshing to know that regardless of my uncertain moments, believing is possible. I am loving the fact that I have found some sure principles for why I can't stop believing.

1. *God's Presence!* He is everywhere. Psalms 139:5-10[1] gives me what I need, daily, to acknowledge His presence and trust it in my life. This helps me know that God is always with me, and to know Him is to trust Him.
2. *God's Power!* Matthew 19:26[2] encourages me to embrace that there is nothing my God cannot do. It is empowering to know that not only does God have the ability, but He also has the desire. Ephesians 3:20[3] assures me that my God can exceed in abundance all I could ever ask.
3. *God's Promises.* No matter where I am in the process, it's all to get me to God's promise. Hebrews 6:17[4] is where I anchor my belief in God's promises. One of my favorite scriptures is Jeremiah 29:11[5], as believing God births assurance. He promises that He has a plan for me that is not a disaster.
4. *God's Peace.* I have learned to keep believing because of God's peace. In those moments of disappointment, pain, uncertainty, and all of the above, I am grateful for God's peace! It has been the byproduct of me trusting God. Philippians 4:7[6] has aided in my process of having a peace that passes all understanding while I hold on to what I believe.

I can't stop believing!

—*Your Sister Who is No Longer Doubting*

---

[1] *Psalms 139:5-10 GNT:* [5] You are all around me on every side; you protect me with your power. [6] Your knowledge of me is too deep; it is beyond my understanding. [7] Where could I go to escape from you? Where could I get away from your presence? [8] If I went up to heaven, you would be there; if I lay down in the world of the dead, you would be there. [9] If I flew away beyond the east or lived in the farthest place in the west, [10] you would be there to lead me, you would be there to help me.

[2] *Matthew 19:26 GNT:* Jesus looked straight at them and answered, "This is impossible for human beings, but for God everything is possible."

[3] *Ephesians 3:20 KJV:* Now unto him that is able to do exceeding abundantly above all that we ask or think, according to the power that worketh in us,

[4] *Hebrews 6:17 NIV:* Because God wanted to make the unchanging nature of his purpose very clear to the heirs of what was promised, he confirmed it with an oath.

[5] *Jeremiah 29:11 KJV:* For I know the thoughts that I think toward you, saith the LORD, thoughts of peace, and not of evil, to give you an expected end.

[6] *Philippians 4:7 GNT:* And God's peace, which is far beyond human understanding, will keep your hearts and minds safe in union with Christ Jesus.

My Sweet Sister,

I've got some questions I've been meaning to ask you:
- Who has hindered you?
- What is it that made you give up on life?
- What caused you to forget that you were more than the total of what you could see in the mirror?
- Who caused you to shrink back from who you are?
- Why did you give up after the diagnosis? It wasn't terminal. It just meant a different way of living, not that you had to stop living. It bothers me that you didn't seek to go beyond the label of the diagnosis, so again, who has hindered you? And what is preventing you from overcoming?

My Sweet Sister,

I've seen you overcome way more. What about this is different? What about made you throw in the towel? I've seen you leap tall buildings to save others, to love them, to extend compassion, to extend grace to them. What has caused you to not be able to pull up the distant memories of the great profession you had chosen? Why didn't you finish college? What caused you never to buy the house, never to learn to drive, never take the trip? What caused you to think that you were not good enough nor smart enough? Who told you that you were not created uniquely purposed, and why did you believe them? Who told you that you could not overcome, that you could not get through, that you could not jump the hurdle and stay in the race? What made you stop, sis? Was it the wrong relationship? The toxic interaction of one who had destined himself to all kinds of misery? Was it the label of a harsh mother or a father who should have loved you but instead despised your birth? You must remember that others' issues have nothing to do with who you are.

What made you let go of life and let go of the smile; let go of the last of the boisterous laughter that makes everyone else laugh in concert with you? What made you let go of the unique relationships with people who only meant to love you and make sure things were well with you. What caused you to allow bitterness to take the place of happiness? Who told you that you were weak, life was worthless, and you could never be happy? You can, if you are willing, and you will.

You see, Sister:

I've seen you and your determination to get things done, and I know this is something you can do. Square your shoulders, stick out your chest, straighten your back, and walk in the authority given to you; it is your birthright. Your divine designer made you to be the greatest, but you are letting life pass you by.

Long before the pandemic, you chose to build a wall to protect yourself that has now caged you in. Take the determination you use to be miserable and turn it around: Use that same determination to live, to have joy, to walk in who you are. You are loving, kind, compassionate. Let somebody in; open the windows, throw back the shutters, and let in the fresh air—the breath of life—and breathe. Get out of the cage; come out of the shell. They're not protecting you.

The walls of your protection have become the makings of your prison, and the only one that has the key is you. Unlock the door and open it up. Life awaits. The diagnosis may still there, the challenges may always be there, but if you are willing to open the door, there will be someone to love you, serve you, have compassion and extend to you what you once extended to others. What you want has always been before you.

Why did you give up on life? Why did you let go?

Whoever told you to let go, whoever told you that you were worthless, whomever it was that told you, they lied.

—You Might Have Been Held Up, but Don't Be Backed Up

Dear Bitter, Sweet Sister

DEAR BITTER, SWEET SISTER,

"I've fallen, and I can't get up!" rings in my head regularly.

After suffering a major injury due to a failed surgery, there are moments where I literally fall and can't get up. Progression in my recovery has been bitter-sweet. I am extremely grateful for the progress and thankful that it's not worse, but I often wonder what happened. Was the surgeon that tired, nervous, or overtaken by the pressures of his own personal/professional life at the time? Did something startle him? Was he careless, or is this the result of human error? It's all such a mystery, and it's extremely rare, but the outcome and life-altering effects are NOT a mystery anymore. Much of the adjustments I've had to make are very much known and visible.

As I continue to press through this journey, it's the fallen moments that have left me overwhelmed and bitter. It seems that every time I fall, I am startled, scared, and sad because the fall reminds me that I'm still broken! It reminds me that—at the hands of a surgeon—I lost an ability that most have not struggled with for three decades of life...I lost the ability to WALK!

These moments are especially bitter for me as I wrestle with the thoughts of how I got here. For a moment, I'm overwhelmed with a sense of bitterness toward the surgeon. I mean, does he understand what I am dealing with now? Years after the surgery, it's a challenge for me to get up and walk daily.

I've fallen so many times; I am concerned I could reinjure myself. Wheeeewwww, what a sense of uncertainty and insecurity! The ongoing treatments, therapy, and efforts to keep me medically comfortable have, on occasion, left me bitter. I use a couple of medical devices that aid in my ability to walk. But I have often asked if all of this could have been avoided? Whether or not, I have finally come to the sweet part of this! I had to forgive the surgeon for whatever went wrong. He is human, and I don't believe what happened to me was an intentional act. I have embraced that my condition has a divine purpose.

I have grown and overcome so many emotions and feelings of inadequacy. I went from being this very energetic, confident, capable, and physically able young woman to a more energetic, confident, limited physical strength, faith-filled, forward-thinking woman. Today, I am better, not bitter. I am amazed, not angry! Why? Because my story could have had so many other narratives, but I chose to embrace the journey, and it was sweet. No longer is it about me wondering *why*. Now, it's about me knowing *what*. What am I supposed to become through this? What areas of my life need to be developed because of something so traumatic?

Having a different perspective and viewing this ordeal through a different lens has caused me to release feelings of bitterness and evolve into a better, sweeter person.

—Your Better, Sweet Sister

Doctor Sister

Hi Dr. M!

I hope this letter finds you well and brightens your day.

During the beginning of my search to find a healthcare provider and OBGYN, I knew two things: one, I wanted a female doctor, and two, I wanted someone I could trust and someone pleasant. Much of my experiences with doctors was very traumatic before we met each other. I saw multiply doctors, both male and female, some friendly others not so much. However, meeting you provided a sense of peace I had never experienced in the health care system. This letter is to express my gratitude for your service as my OBGYN and your impact on my life as a patient and woman.

As a woman, my memories of conversations regarding sexuality, sex, and how to navigate my body weren't something spoken about with frequency, ease, or positivity. However, at the start of my visits to your office, you confidently offered medical advice that reminded me of my rights and responsibility as a woman and patient. You've consistently provided a safe space for small talk and exams all in one. Most importantly, you listened to my concerns when I wasn't feeling well. You have always been eager to answer questions when I have been unsettled regarding medical decisions. You have also been stern when needing to give advice that warranted my focus.

I have a memory of one of the many visits to your office. You noticed something different in my demeanor. During this visit, I shared with you the passing of my grandmother, the incarceration of my father, lack of sleep, intense drinking, etc. You immediately shifted gears on how these visits are usually tailored and allowed me to cry and continue to talk. Afterward, you prayed with me, helped me calm down, and refocus myself, and then offered advice for the next steps to take. With every appointment after that, you've always taken time during my appointments to check-in with me. You still encourage me and remind me to always be medically conscious and only engage in safe sex.

Over the past 10 years plus, I've expressed to my family and friends how grateful I am to have you in my life. For me, having you as an OBGYN is a bonus to the years of care you've provided before ever administering test results, conducting exams, or writing prescriptions.

Dr. M, you are far more than an OBGYN: I believe the medical field is the vehicle in which you, and maybe even God, chose to spread love and light to women as they walk in and out of your office. Know that you are appreciated far beyond what you may see, think, or feel after a long day. The world needs more OBGYN's like you on the front line and within our communities to educate, empower, and enrich women.

Because of your medical transparency and the way you care for your patients, I have been more responsible and aware of myself as a patient and woman. I've become more open about challenges and more articulate when communicating my needs as a woman without shame.

Dr. M,
Thank You!

Open Wounds that Cut Me Deep

Sunflower in Libra

SUNFLOWER IN LIBRA,

Who knows if you will see this?
Heck! Who knows if you will even know it's for you?
Either way, here goes:

The hardest part of writing this letter is admitting that you truly were the love of my life. You were the one I saw myself spending forever with, ten times over. You were the one who helped me remember me.

I remember the first time I felt more than just a friendship with you. It was the day you said, "Dude, do you know who you are?!?" It wasn't what you said so much as how you said it. You legit believed what you were saying.

It meant a lot to me that you cared.

You saw something in me that I was starting to forget and needed to remember at that exact time. I was more vulnerable with you than I had ever been with anyone, ever. I shared things with you that I never shared with anyone else. I cried tears with you that I truly believed you would hold WITH me, not for me.

I remember that night, when it was all shot to pieces; you and my EX-best friend thought I suspected that something was going on between you two, but that couldn't have been the furthest thing from my mind. I literally said nothing, and both of you flipped on me because of my silence. That was weird—guilt-ridden and weird. Anyway, once all of that was said and done, and we tried to connect again, you saying to me, "Don't tell anyone that we've connected or are speaking again," made me realize that you knew you had said things that weren't true about me and done things to me that I didn't deserve. It's one thing to have a disagreement with someone; it's another to assassinate someone's character.

I wanted to marry you. I even had the proposal outlined in my head. It was going to be some Martin proposing to Gina type ish. Heck, my mom loved and still loves you, which says a lot. I'm sure she knew we were together; she still asks about you from time to time. I just say, "She's well," and I change the subject.

Either way, I have no regrets.

I don't hate you. In fact, I still love you, as crazy as that may sound. My prayer is that you don't hate me. If you do, I pray that one day you won't. If you never do, it was just meant for me to be the big bad wolf in your story, and that's okay; my intentions were always genuine with you, even if it didn't seem like it.

I know there's still some healing that needs to take place. I sometimes wish we could talk, though, and just reminisce about the good times. I know I didn't do everything right, and there are times I could have made better decisions, but my intentions were always pure.

I wish you well and pray you achieve, and smash, every goal you've set for yourself. I saw greatness in you from the first time we met. In the meantime, keep going, keep pushing, and I pray you never lose sight of yourself, especially in someone else.

IN LOVE,
Aquarius

I Was Scared

To My Sisters Who I Could Not Help,

I want to say, "I'm sorry," to those of you I encountered who were battered and broken at the hands of another. I am sorry I did not move to action. I am sorry I could not help. I am sorry I did not enter the space of your suffering at the moment when you were experiencing the abuse.

To the Mother of Two Next Door Who Lived with the Violently Abusive and Sadistic Man:

I am sorry that I could not move. I heard the devastation. I heard all his anger being poured out on you his wrath, the evil being perpetrated against you. I am so sorry I could not respond.

You see, there is no way to know exactly what another sister is going through. I could not imagine why you were so mean, appeared so miserable, or why you would not interact with other people. I thought it strange when I smiled and waved—and said hello—and you did not respond. I just didn't know. Yeah, I was a kid, but I still judged you for it because I didn't know.

I'm sorry that when you screamed that he might kill you, I could not move on the other side of that wall, alone. I was paralyzed with fear and terrified you would find out that I knew what was going on.

You, too, had no way of knowing that I grew up in a household where domestic violence was commonplace. My father, who at that time was addicted to drugs, was also violent toward my mother. You had no idea about the many times I couldn't sleep at night. I would lie there paralyzed with fear, thinking he might kill my mother or permanently injure or disfigure her. You had no way to know about the time when my mom was forced to jump out the second-story window to escape him in the middle of the night with a knife in her hand. You knew nothing of those things.

Please know I wanted so badly to respond. I just didn't know how. I wanted to save you, but I didn't know what to do. It wasn't that I didn't want to; I couldn't. I could not bring my body to move. I could not make my young limbs get out of bed to find the phone and call the police on your behalf.

To the Sister Whose Husband of Your Youth Hit You in the Face and Knocked You to the Ground:

I apologize because I could not move to save you.

I am sorry that no one else would help you. I'm sorry your husband's friend watched and did nothing. He appeared to be just as frightened of your husband as you were. After that, your husband simply picked you up off the ground and put you in his car.

I wonder what happened to you just the same as I wonder what happened to the lady next door.

I often wonder about the sisters I saw who were afraid to voice their opinions. Because of their family norms, they were afraid to speak up for themselves, afraid to end the abuse.

To the Other Women in my Neighborhood:

Growing up, I watched some of you become so accustomed to the abuse that you developed signals so neighbors nearby would know you needed assistance. I'm sorry I couldn't rescue you. I am sorry I could not help.

All these years later, it grieves me to think that some of you may not even be free now. Some of you may still be existing in those toxic environments. Maybe you stayed because you did not have the chance to get away and rebuild, or maybe you did not think leaving was safer. Was it under the threat of death that you stayed? Maybe it was because you did not want to bring anyone else harm.

I will never know.

To Each of You, My Abused Sisters:

I'm sorry I could not save you or offer resources to help you flee. There are no real words to soothe, comfort, or motivate you to finally leave. I am sorry for the cycles now passed on to your children and the ill-expressed anger that will flow to your children's children. Thinking about each of you still makes me pray more at night; you make me reflect in those quiet moments. I'm sorry. I couldn't help. I was just a little girl, but now—as a woman—I still feel the aftermath. The effect still lingers deep in my soul.

It's a tragedy that domestic abuse is commonplace, so I offer words of encouragement and hope for women and men in circumstances like yours. These words are for those who have endured and who have survived. I want you to know I am rooting for you, and I commit to working with you to find resources even as I assist others in the same situations.

I am sorry, Sisters. I pray you have found freedom and that you will know life, laughter, and love. You should not be ashamed. Be empowered to walk in the spirit of joy because you were created to live in joy, and you deserve it.

—Please Forgive Me for My Silence

I'm Angry

Dear Mama,

I'm angry. I'm anxious. Often, feelings of agony overcome my body just at the thought of how alone I've been throughout my life. I've experienced so much discomfort with every relationship I've encountered, including ours.

Since the age of fifteen—when you exiled me from the house—I've always felt displaced, never really belonging to anything or anyone. You see, I assumed my relationship with you would be wrapped in ribbons of safety, peace, and belonging—where I would experience love, affirmation, and care. However, as time progressed, I felt as though life tore us further apart.

Life as a teenager was challenging enough, but once I was put out of the house, I fell into a deep depression. Therefore, I drowned myself in my education because that was the only space that made me feel valued. Later, I engaged in relationships (in which I stayed longer than I should've) with men who saw my insecurities and exploited them by giving me what I wanted. For many nights, I cried. I felt alone, yet somehow, I managed to still feel loved. I aimed to please you and the girls only to end up feeling empty with my faith shaken. I experienced many nights of physical, verbal, and emotional abuse.

Mama,

I'm sure you are wondering why I never mentioned any of this before now. Well, the truth is, I never felt I could say any of this to you;

I never felt as though I was worthy of sharing my feelings or experiences. When I went to college, I never felt supported and endured many days without the things I truly needed.

After graduate school, I again moved with a guy I was dating at the time. I allowed myself to trust a woman I'd met at my workplace at the time; this person betrayed me and used the information she'd learned about me to punish me. She shared my personals with others in a way that wasn't healthy. I ended up losing my job; I experienced depression flares, weight gain, hair loss, and so much pain. I needed your support, your love, guidance, and affirmation.

Every decision I've made until now has been to please you and get your attention; I yearned for some type of assurance from you that my life was worthy. The little girl in me needed your guidance and still yearns for motherly support.

You need to know that I blamed you for the abuse I endured. I blame you for the failure of my sisters and the relationship we never cultivated from our youth. I blame you for my lack of sensuality, sexuality, and security. As a young girl and even as a woman, I've endured body image discomfort, humiliation, aggression, and desperation. These are difficulties that I grow through every day now, yet I hope we can reconnect and be open to the work that is needed for us to have a healthy relationship.

The truth is, Mama, although I have carried a deeply rooted anguish toward you, I do love YOU! My anger has softened. I am now ready to heal in ways that allow me to open up to you—and me—again.

MAMA,
Let us connect and do this work, together.

—Missing You and Missing a Piece of Me

To the Baddest Chicks

To the Baddest Chicks:

One of the most challenging things for me to learn was how to take responsibility for my part in some of the personal misfortune I've experienced. You chicks were instrumental to that learning.

I learned a lot from your strengths and your confident demeanor. For that, I applaud you. I affectionately refer to you as "The Baddest Chicks" because you are one the most efficient at what you do. There is something to be commended about women who get it done against all the odds.

I do have a question though: Is there a line in the sand that you will not cross to give the appearance that you are always the winner, the one who can do what someone else could not?

To the Baddest Chicks:

Different settings require us to move in different ways, and women often work harder while receiving less compensation. We are not viewed nor treated as equals. Our opinions and proposals are overlooked. Our voices are muted, yet—mediocrity being unacceptable—we stop making excuses, and we make moves. We get it done.

Personally, I get it in the boss up: the practice of securing the bag in this world in which we live. However, I refuse to embrace the philosophy that other women must be nullified and brought low for one woman to succeed. No woman's candle should have to be publicly snuffed out for yours to continue to shine.

Let Your Phenomenal Womanhood Speak for Itself.

When you spend time committing to projects and ideas, you raise the bar and set the standard for what is brought to the table. It is a joy and blessing to watch your brilliance unfold. Yet, it's an absolute catastrophe to watch you bulldoze and criticize other women whose perspectives or experiences are different than yours. Being firm is not wrong, but cruelly humiliating others is. Love corrects and teaches with care, engages with compassion, and desires to encourage growth even when leading with a hard lesson. My prayer is that you will find your way there.

To the Baddest:

A word of caution: what you sow, you will reap. All of us do.

Your extraordinary gifting enamors and benefits the work, lives, and reputations of others. I cheer you on from a distance as I pray: I hope your capacity to hear a voice with another tenor and tone will increase. The perceptions of others must be respected rather than diminished or silenced. Your victory is sure; the bag is already secured, but each of us can be our greatest strength and our most significant liability. There is an inherent danger in performing so well: someone will always need and seek your expertise while ignoring the abrasions you inflict. Once, that someone was me.

The pain is excruciating. The sting of it still real. In time, this too will heal.

The tools and strategies used to expose the issues and failures of others reveal yours too. It appears you have forgotten to remember this fact. Please do. We could have shared this conversational exchange, but you are not ready to hear what you are quick to say to others.

The company, organization, or job will always be better because you were there. It is undeniable. Just know that carnage and casualty are not necessary for your victory.

—You Have Already Won

Family Tragedies

In the Living Room

To My Dear Sister,

On this day, you sat in the living room as you usually would've. I think you were about eight or nine years old. You were so innocent and pure and good. Your intuition has always been strong. Your will has always been even stronger. You were also alone and an outcast because you were different.

Even as a young girl, you knew what was right and what was wrong. The adults in the house were so were twisted, and your spirit recognized it. Baby sister, that is why they didn't want you around. When they told you that you talked too much, they really meant you saw too much. The more you saw, the more they wanted to silence you. And silence you, they did. They constantly reinforced in you all the negative things about you that they thought would shut you up. But oh, baby! I remember that made your discernment even stronger as you continued to speak out about the things you saw, especially what you weren't supposed to see or know.

Someone should have been your advocate in that house. Someone should have told you it was okay to be confident! Someone should have told you not to doubt yourself and reaffirm that what you saw was real. Someone should have been there to protect you. But baby sister, I am so glad those things you saw made you so strong. Baby sister, I am so glad they didn't break your spirit. Baby sister, I am so glad you didn't turn out like them. I am so glad you had enough endurance to stand no matter what.

That day in the living room, when he told you to come sit on his lap, I saw you sit down, and I saw him touch you. Somebody passed by in the hallway as it happened, and they saw you too. For a minute, you sat there. Then suddenly, something clicked in your head, and you knew you had to get away. You see, baby sister, it was a rite of passage for the others before you. But you, in that moment, knew it was wrong. You jumped up off his lap, but you didn't speak a word. THEY HAD SILENCED YOU! But there was someone that knew what would happen next and she SAVED YOU!

Baby Sister,

Just know there was someone in the shadows that loved you, that knew she couldn't let you be a victim of what was to come if you stayed. Baby sister, she had to let you go. It was the only way to SAVE you.

My Dear Baby Sister,

You were right in every way. Never allow anyone to silence you again. Never allow outside influences to make you feel like you are not worthy. Baby sister, just know you were never alone, and the separation was a necessity for your growth and development. God has always had his hands on you, and, to this day, he has never left you. Sister, embrace your story and let it be your driving force to be great and greater than you witnessed growing up. That young girl you were—watching and dealing with grown people's issues—helped mold you into the woman you are today.

SISTER, YOU HAVE THE POWER TO SPEAK TO THOSE GENERATIONAL CURSES!

SISTER, OPEN YOUR MOUTH AND LIVE!

—Your Angel in Disguise

Should Have Loved You More

MY DEAR SISTER,

Oh, how I miss you.

I must first say that I am sorry I didn't love you enough while you were here. I am sorry I was sometimes ashamed of you. I never thought I was better than you, but sometimes I was embarrassed by you. I thought you could have carried yourself better than how you did. I loved you, but I should have shown you more. If there is one thing I regret in this life, it is not showing you enough love.

I always had your back since I was sixteen years old, but the older I got, the more space was put between us. I remember when you had your first child; we were living in the same apartment complex. I was living with auntie, and you had your own apartment by that time. I remember purchasing diapers for him; he was my first nephew, and he was such a sweet boy. I remember you doing the best that you could. At the same time, you were battling demons. As a child, I couldn't understand the things you were dealing with, and the people around us often gave in to the folly at your expense.

I am sorry that as I grew up, I didn't defend you more. The older I became, the more I realized that you had been hurt so much that you had to struggle just to stay sane. I'm sorry I judged you so much. I'm sorry I looked over you at times. When I became grown, I'm sorry that I didn't invite you to hang out with me more than I asked you to watch my kids.

This letter makes me seem like an awful little sister to you. It makes me want to run down the list of good things I have done for you and tell people that I was a great asset to you, but it only would be to ease the pain I feel for not showing you enough love while you were here with me on Earth.

SISTER,

I shed tears as I read through this letter to you. Not knowing how much pain I felt, I don't think I can say I'm sorry enough! I know you knew I LOVED you, but in hindsight, I wish I showed you more on this side of glory. I pray your spirit will receive this and forgive me. With this letter, I pray that I can begin to heal and forgive myself for not loving you enough.

It was I who had to receive your body back from Arizona after your death. I remember getting the call from two of our other sisters with your husband on the phone. It was 1:30 a.m. on July 19, 2014. I remember calling up the stairs to my husband in disbelief. He held me as I screamed, "NOOO! NOOO! NOOO."

Never again will I let those who I love go about without knowing that I love them. Because of you, I will love harder and show it. Because of you, I will be more empathetic and less judgmental. Your heart was like no other person on Earth. You were such a kind soul that many, including our mother, took advantage of. You endured so much. It probably would have killed me to bear even the tip of the trials you faced.

MY SISTER:

I love you today, and yesterday I should have shown you how much.

—I Love You, and I Miss Ya

Dear Niece

Dear Niece,

There is so much I want to tell you and so much I want to explain. I genuinely wish I could take back the years I've missed with you. The time that aunties spend getting to know their nieces and nephews. I had the opportunity to but just didn't.

The truth is I was scared, and I'm still scared. The truth is that I let my fear of losing you keep me away from you. I thought that my sexuality and the beliefs of your parents would keep us apart. It's not that I thought they would keep me away from you or turn me away; we just have differences in opinion about life and how to live it. I guess my biggest fear was that if it turned out that you like women, I would get blamed. That's crazy, right?

Niece,

It's amazing how crippling fear can be—how it can literally take over your whole existence and stop you from things you can never get back. Time is the one thing I wish I could get back with you and your brother. What's funny is, I know I would have been the coolest aunt ever. I would have loved every minute of hanging out and getting to know the person you are. I hate that I have missed out on major parts of your life. My prayer is that one day we can talk about all of this. I also pray that you don't hold it against me.

I take full blame for allowing my fears to dictate our relationship. I guess it goes back further than I know how to explain. Our family hasn't always been the most accepting or welcoming to anything outside of tradition—which, of course, leads to self-imposed fear and made-up scenarios that don't exist. Couple this with comments made by other family members and... I can't deal.

I don't know if you know this, but one of the cousins said something very damaging to me a while ago, and unfortunately, I've lived with that in the back of my mind ever since. I buried it deep in the depths of my heart, and in turn, I've shut off certain parts of me—not only from family but from the world. I told myself that because my cousin felt that way, my whole family would.

I also regret not spending time with your mom. Maybe fear has been the driving force between her and I as well. I wish we had a regular sister-sister relationship. But then again, what is regular? Maybe one day, she and I will be able to truly connect and talk about all of this.

In the meantime, I want you to know that I am truly proud of you. I know you will make a change in this world, and auntie will be right there cheering you on. I can't wait to see how you will make your mark and show the world who you are. I genuinely hope and pray you know how much auntie loves you and how very proud I am to call you my niece.

I love you.

Love,
Tee-Tee

One Child I Left Behind

TO THE CHILD I WAS FORCED TO LEAVE BEHIND:

Before you, I wasn't unfamiliar with feelings of shame, with my entire existence being the result of a love affair between my mother and father. My sisters were distraught and disheartened by the fact that my mother boasted in my birth while battling a mental health condition and her addiction to my father.

When my mother died, I was the young and tender age of 15—broken and alone—and passed around to live with family members. After being bussed to my sister's place in another state, I hoped for a better life with my siblings' help and guidance. Once I arrived, I quickly realized my pregnancy just brought more shame to my family.

My oldest sister felt that the best way to help was to convince me to sign over my parental rights, and when you got older, she'd help me explain everything to you. It wasn't until later that I learned she'd never intended to stick with our agreement, and she had her own plan in motion.

I was a child myself at this moment, making an adult decision that I wasn't proud of, but I believed it was the only option. So, as you got older, although we lived in the same city, my sister didn't allow me to communicate with you. She raised you as if I don't exist and never acknowledges that I am your biological mother. I know this was hard to understand as a child, and I am deeply sorry that you felt anger, disappointment, neglect, and sadness because of it.

As I got older and began to have other children, I still created a space in my heart and life for you. I watched you grow older and accomplish many milestones—milestones I wasn't present for—and, for that, I apologize too. I now know that you weren't permitted to acknowledge me as your mother, and I wasn't always sure how to support you. I didn't want to discredit the love and support given to you by my sister and her husband. They were able to provide a life for you in ways I would never have been able to match. I was also able to provide them the opportunity to be parents, which was a long-awaited wish of my sisters, so I guess that's a plus.

Many times, this felt like a battle—one that I lost, and my sister won—because I never felt supported or accepted by her. Despite all this, just know I love you with every ounce of life in my body, and I have always desired the best for you. I pray for you constantly, and I am extremely proud to be your mother and friend.

—*Your Mother, Your Sister, and Your Friend*

Untitled

HELLO LADY V,

It's me, your granddaughter.

It bothers me that I only have one memory of you being around as a child. This memory is only present because of old family photos and tapes of my third birthday party. I wasn't always privy to many details about you, my aunt, or even my Mom and Dad's relationship. I must admit that I have days when I wonder why I don't have a relationship with you. Other days, it's a distant thought—out of sight, out of mind.

You've been absent for many milestones in my life, and I was left in the dark with unanswered questions, unattended emotions, watching you care for my siblings. When I permit myself to feel everything that comes with feeling disappointed and abandoned, I get angry. I wonder how a woman of faith professes such love.

See, you profess to love, and yet you neglect your flesh and blood. You condone a father being negligent to his seed. You favor a man who fathered many children and never owned his responsibilities as a man and father. As a woman who initially raised her children alone, why would you repeat the cycle with your son? Did you not consider the hurt and pain it caused you both?

My mother altered her life so she could provide for and nurture her child. She sacrificed her time and dreams to provide the best childhood filled with faith, family, fellowship, and a community of love. Her example made me realize that to live a life of joy, peace, and abundance, I needed to forgive you.

Therefore, my prayer for you is that you will seek the help you need to confront your traumas.

I forgive you, your son, and your daughter.

You see, I chose a few years ago to forgive you and move forward. However, it wasn't easy. I realized my learning to forgive, sooner rather than later, opens doors to living a life of love, happiness. Forgiveness helped me cultivate a network of those who gracefully and excitedly want to be a part of my life. Although you chose not to be a part of mine for selfish reasons, God has blessed me with a community that thrives on love and peace.

So much has happened since my third birthday. I've blossomed into an amazing young lady. Outside of studying, I enjoy writing, blogging, photography, and other activities that take all of me to create.

I invite you to get to know me and cultivate a relationship if you choose. I only ask that you be open to the truth and transparency of who you are, the questions I have about my childhood, and discussion on how we can move forward.

—Forgiven, but Not Forgotten

Missing Father

TO THE WOMAN MISSING HER FATHER,

I still cry when I think about my Dad leaving me. Maybe it is for all the tears I did not cry when it happened. Even though he was my grandfather, he was the only example of a father that I ever had. I live with the memory of losing him so vividly—sometimes, I hold it closer than memories of him being here. I remember what it was like walking those long hospital hallways knowing he wasn't coming home.

I still try to figure out how the quietest place in the hospital was the most painful. You expect pain to have a sound, but there was no sound there. Maybe that is why I learned to suffer in silence; the greatest pain I ever felt did not have a sound. There was a stillness in the hospital air, not the kind that peace brings, but the stillness that comes in moments when the second hand freezes on a clock. Time stood still, and if I did not know any better, I would say a part of my heart stopped beating the same way yours did.

It has been thirteen years now. I remember nurses walking my uncle, my cousin, and I to a specific location but giving us directions as if to say we would have to find our own way. As we passed all those windowless closed doors with light creeping out from under them, I remember thinking that I was going to a special room to wait until I could see him. Finally, we got to an open door only to find my mama sitting in front of a phone book. Who could she possibly be calling? "What's wrong?" we asked. Her pause lasted long enough only for the nurse who had been sitting with her to leave the room.

Mama pulled us kids in close. I remember her words like it was yesterday. "You know we took good care of your granddaddy, and he's been sick for a while. Well, he just couldn't make it."

I heard her, and I was silent. My cousin bolted out of the door and down the hospital halls as if he were going to look for our patriarch to bring granddaddy back himself. They went after my cousin. I walked to those two black chairs against the waiting room wall and sat on my hands; I was numb. I sat there and waited. I did not want to believe it. I just knew my granddaddy would not leave me. I knew he was coming home.

In that moment, everyone was so consumed in their own grief the way they had always been so consumed in their own life. As I sat there on my hands, I heard them tell mama, "She's young. She doesn't understand it." Since I never cried, they did not realize I had just lost my best friend.

Everyone eventually made it back to this white-washed room that felt like a box. The nurses took us to some unknown part of the hospital, and there he was. I had seen him in so many hospital beds in life that I just sat there and waited on him to move. I waited on his eyes to open, yet they never did. I stood at his feet and waited on him to ask for his baseball cap because I knew he was so ready to go. Daddy never moved. He hated hospitals, so he wanted to be home teaching me how to work the computer. I just knew he was coming home.

The next week of our lives would be so different. People flooded our house—that no longer felt the same—every day. The door would open, and I would look up, expecting it to be him. I knew he would soon come in and tell us that they finally got the pacemaker in and working so he could come home. When we did not answer the house phone, his voice would play on the recording. I still had not cried because he still had a chance to come home.

Then Tuesday came, and everybody got dressed. We got into these limos. It was my first time in a limo, so I wanted to tell my daddy all about it. We took this long quiet ride to the funeral home. It was a place I had never been to. And those were words I had never heard before, so I did not know what to expect. We walked in, and there daddy was, lying in some crazy-looking box with his legs closed off. He had on clothes he would never wear. Where were his suspenders?

Where were his khaki pants and his baseball cap to keep his head warm? Why wasn't he up, raising sand, telling people he wanted to come home? I sat in the chair by the door and watched everyone cry; my face was still dry.

The next morning, we loaded back in those limos, and they circled the church parking lot. We marched down the aisle of the church while they played the saddest music in the world. I kept wondering why all these people were standing on the sides of us, watching us like we were on a television show. I remember getting to the end of that aisle, and there daddy was, still lying in this thing. I just knew he was ready to get up. I sat on the front row of that church next to mama as people filed by. When the line was over, they started closing that box down on him. Tears started to fill my eyes, and the next thing I knew, they were rolling down my cheeks the way rain falls off the rooftop in summer thunderstorms. Daddy was not coming home.

I collapsed on my mama's lap. Who was going to hold my hand now? Who was going to sit outside while I rode my bicycle and pretended to do tricks all in Mama's garden? He was supposed to buy me my first cell phone and my first car. Who was going to take care of me now? People got up and down from that podium. It all seemed so big from where I was sitting. The rest of that day is such a blur.

Lady,

I was eleven years old when my daddy left, and that hole is still as fresh as the smell of grass chopped down in the morning. He is missed so much. I get angry at him sometimes when I look at where we are and how often we struggled since he's been gone. I wonder, "Why couldn't you have held on just a little bit longer?" Didn't he know how bad we needed him?

Sometimes, it feels like he left me here, unprotected. He never taught me how to live without him. Every time something crazy in life happens, I find myself saying it would not have been if he had just been here. He would have saved me. I so desperately miss holding his hand as a little girl. I miss him picking me up to keep me away from danger. I miss the sound of hearing his truck turn into the yard. He taught me what love was in the form of safety, and I have looked for the safety of his love in so many places.

So, to you, my sister, who has lost the first man you ever learned to love: It gets better. While they may not be here in the physical, they know who they raised you to become, and you know who they raised you to be. Grief is not something you get over; it is something we get through day by day. Some days are easier than others, and some days, I just want to hear him tell me, "Good Job."

I wonder if I made him proud, but I know I did. He thought I could be anything, and some days, I just need to have the confidence in myself that he had in me. I miss him the way trees miss leaves in winter, but I just keep going, and sister, you can too.

—Missing My Daddy

Situations That Left Me Undone

I Never Wanted You

HEY BABY,

I can't believe I left you there.

I can't believe I was left in quite a situation myself.

What about my life at the time created a situation where I found myself in a line, by myself, for an abortion, responding to a pregnancy that I did not plan?

What did I do to be chosen for such nonsense?

What I DO know is that I killed you, and that... well, that's just it. I don't even know what to say.

I don't know who I would be, or who you would be, or what would have happened to our life together, but it was the decision I made based on the condition I was in. Honestly, if I had to do it all over again, I would do the same thing.

I wasn't ready for you back then. I wasn't even ready for me. If I had known I would end up PREGNANT, I never would have had sex with him in the first place, but... it wasn't at all that simple—not at all that simple.

I never knew that guys—MEN—are really out here TRYING to get women pregnant ON PURPOSE without their consent! We know what we equate with rape, but what do you call THIS??! Why did I have to be THAT girl? Why did he have to be THAT guy? And why did YOU have to suffer because of the decisions that BOTH of us made?

The more I think, the more questions I have. How has my life been cursed because of my decision? How has my life been blessed because of it? My darling baby, if I spend too much time thinking about it, I won't leave you where you belong—in heaven, in peace.

You see, many years ago, I was a different person. I was attempting to break off my stable life experiences and venture out into something new. I can't quite tell you what all was going through my head at the time, but I knew I wanted something different; I knew I needed change. Essentially, I was looking for love.

It's amazing the things we do in search of love. It seems so simple now, or even cliche, but the relationship I was in prior to meeting THIS guy just wasn't working, and I knew I needed something new. I need to bounce back from a seemingly good situation that wasn't at all good for me. At the time, love wasn't quite what I was looking for, but affection was. I wanted someone to be interested in me. I wanted someone to pay attention to me. I wanted someone to validate me and tell me I am beautiful. I guess that's what I wanted, or at least it's what I thought I needed. Either way, I guess I found that person.

I found a man who I thought was... Well, I don't know what I thought about him. The predicament that he left me in kind of blurs whatever positive view I might have had of him before the episode. Whatever he was or whoever he was, I hate to admit that he had created a space I could feel safe in. I guess I felt too safe: so safe that he could take advantage of me when I was in the most vulnerable state a woman could ever be in... naked... wide open... having sex.

In the heat of the moment, I just HAPPENED to look down (THANK YOU, GOD!), and the condom was OFF. I was shocked! I was BEYOND shocked, in fact! So shocked that whatever I blurted out at the time verbalized how SHOOK I was, and he responded sooooooooooo casually by saying, "Oh, the condom broke." (In this VERY moment, I wish HE were BROKE, but I digress.)

The second time we had sex, the condom just happened to break AGAIN! By this point, I freaked OUT! I was in a state of shock, and I LOST it! I mean, I REALLY lost it. I had never lost it before, and I have never lost it like that again since, but my mind was GONE! I couldn't believe somebody would put me in that situation—ME! I couldn't believe somebody would do that in the first place to ANYBODY. All of my supposed identity just came crashing and tumbling down, and humility hit me like a ton of bricks. Above anything else that had happened in my life before then, that experience made me feel basic. I felt like nobody. I felt like I never had control. I felt completely and UTTERLY naked... wide open... and excessively female.

Only a female would have to endure such drama. Only a female would be in such a predicament as to have to wear someone else's intention for 9 months. Only a woman would have to bear the shame, to carry that weight, to carry the burden—physically, emotionally, financially—that someone else chose for her. It's one thing to have to deal with the problems I create for myself. It's an entirely different consideration to live a life where—because of who I am anatomically—it creates a condition for my organs to be used in ways that someone else chooses—CASUALLY—on my behalf.

What on Earth is that? What kind of tragedy is THIS? What kind of world have I been forced to live in according to what someone else dictates for me based on the very essence of my being? I tire of having to consider one of humanity's most enduring questions:

Who is in control?
Is it me?
Or is it a man?

—I Lost It, I Lost Control, and That's When I Found Me

Little Girl Lost

My Amazing Sister,

Can I tell you about a young teenage girl: small in the waist, flat stomach, fit thick in the thighs with junk in the trunk, and a pretty smile? These were the attributes that garnered the attention of boys who were older and cooler than her classmates. These were the attributes of a teenage girl who was longing for someone—anyone—to make her feel wanted and special.

She found the guy. She thought of him, smiling fondly. "He likes me too." He was too old, but he was popular with just enough charm for a naïve girl who needed the attention. He had to know she was more mature than her age suggested, so maybe they could just have great conversation and hang out with his friends? She had to get him. Inserting herself at just the right time and the right place meant he would take notice.

Him seeing her turned into a walk in the crisp winter evening that would lead to the humiliation and embarrassment of an uninvited sexual encounter she certainly was not ready to have. This involved a different kind of pain she had not experienced. She didn't consent, but she did not scream or fight; she just laid quietly, wishing it to be over. Confused and hurting, she wondered about the contradiction between the nice mannerable guy and what he was hastily trying to accomplish with no regard for her.

He stopped, unsatisfied.

The shame of being ridiculed by him for not being knowledgeable or sexually advanced was crushing. She was left to get up and get herself together with no concern for the sacrificial rendering of her tender heart and virginity. "I gave it all for you to like me more," she thought as he walked her back to the community center. "I wanted him to want me. I wanted him to spend time with me and get to know me." Instead, her desires resulted in more rejection. After the encounter, now, she would be ignored and cast to the side, so he could go on to the next one.

The best decision for her after that would have been to walk away. Hadn't she learned to keep what should not be given out? Hadn't she learned not to barter herself for affection and affirming words? Against logic and moral sensibility, the goal became to prove she could learn to do it better: trying to compete for meaningless moments of pleasure and attempts to find something as simple as sweet words, hand-holding, walks home, and the words, "Let me be your boyfriend." But those things never came.

My Amazing Sister,

What happened to me as a teen set the tone for my twenties. Love escaped me every time, no matter what skills I honed. I was always the one admired in the dark: friend by day, desired at night. Countless glances in the mirror felt like shame was stalking me. I was either not pretty enough or not freaky enough. Which one was it? I reasoned I could try harder. The words were never spoken aloud, but they were undoubtedly implied because there was always someone willing to practice with me.

Every morning yielded the heavy weight of shame for what took place the day or night before. Still, none cut so deep as being the young, exploited, and discarded girl, laughed at when walking home with a battered soul and bloodied undergarments on a cruelly cold winter night.

This girl was me for ten miserable years vacillating between side chick, main chick, stranger, or forever friend to some guy and a couple of frequent flyers. I was prodded, poked, and objectified until I could not perceive my own personhood.

Sis,

Please don't get lost.

Do NOT give up your personhood in exchange for anyone or anything, because if that is what it will cost you, IT COSTS TOO MUCH!

—The Woman Who Found Herself Lost No Longer

Sister of Truth

DEAR SISTER OF TRUTH,

I never imagined how our lives would intertwine so closely. Although we have different parents, you became my sister. I looked to you as an inspiration. You were so successful and independent; I thought that was amazing. Sometimes, I felt inadequate as I had not accomplished nearly the things you had. Still, I never let that stop me from genuinely supporting you and cheering you on.

I am so proud of you and the hard work you have put into your life and career. I mean it when I tell you your focus and determination are like no other that I know. When you commit to doing something, anybody can take it to the bank. I love you for your strong mind and stubbornness.

As we grew closer, we began to trust each other more and more. It was an amazing time in our lives. I remember all the days we were at one another's homes, enjoying spending the day with each other. Sometimes, we moved as if we didn't have a care in the world all while balancing the weight of the world on our shoulders. I always felt you handled all things with such grace—a grace I don't think I possess.

Ironically, now we can't share with each other a lot of the memories from that time. I hate that one day I had to be the bearer of bad news that directly affected your life. Often, I wish I would have kept my mouth shut, but I knew you needed to know what was being told to me. I couldn't let you walk around not knowing what was going on around you.

I was reluctant to say anything because I didn't want any part of what would come after. I didn't want to become the villain. My intent was never to hurt you, and I truly wish the information had not been brought to me.

Sister of Truth,

It has been a few years now, and we have all moved on. Still, I often think about what life would be like if I hadn't told you. There was no way to know how you would respond to me or how you would treat me. I have no way of knowing if you would feel some type of way about me keeping the truth from you, but I am grateful that God allowed us to remain stable.

I am grateful I can still call you my sister.

In this life, we don't get it right all the time. In some areas, we will ultimately fail. I am so glad that, in the area of family, we got it right. No matter the decisions we make, we always have each other's back. Space and miles away from each other have not changed a thing between us. Please keep my bed warm when I come to visit.

Thank you for always providing a safe space for me at any given notice. Thank you for always showing up. Never change your heart toward others. It wasn't pretty, but I am so glad to know that no matter the issue, you know I will tell you the truth. And I know you will do the same for me.

I love you, and there is nothing you can do about it.

—VA 2018

Sis, That Was Foul

Sis,

I wish you would have told me that friendship with you was just a glimpse into the world of appearances. Naivety, youthfulness, and the insatiable appetite for attention were the ingredients for the perfect storm waiting to happen. Always the life of the party, dressed to impress, face beat, long legs with short skirts or painted on jeans before skinny jeans were even a thing. Free without responsibility for the weekend, we hit the parties and strolled the campus. If you saw one of us, you were sure to locate the other.

Finally, there came a chance to be with the in-crowd, the cool kids. It was a chance to be one of the desirable people for the first time; we ate that up! It is a curious thing the lengths we go just to feel wanted or to prove to our past that we had indeed surpassed the upbringing, the abandonment, the abuse, or neglect. It wasn't that we *shall* overcome; we knew we had already overcome the stigma of the old neighborhood. It felt delicious to be thought well of and cheered on from the sidelines for choosing to make positive strides. We moved proudly together at that time. Yet...

I didn't know we were supposed to be in competition with each other in the process—silly me. I thought we were riding together. The pain of your betrayal was deep—my reputation was sullied because of the appearance of evil for a scenario that *you* set up. "I did not sleep with that guy! I don't even know him," I explained.

"Hey, girl, please tell my guy who just saw me walking with you that I did not sleep with that boy! I just bumped into you three."

You did not defend my honor and speak well of me. You chose to cause others to think poorly of me.

I remember asking you to consider the pain I would feel if you refused to tell the truth. Still, you chose to let a friend believe I betrayed him so you would not have to reveal you had crossed the sacred code of friendship in a personal attempt to exact revenge. You tried to get back at someone who could not have cared any less. Sure, my character spoke louder than the nasty rumor you set in motion for self-preservation. Those who knew me soon realized the tea was not valid, but why would my beloved sister harm me when you did not have to?

As it turned out, both our issues spoke louder than the awkward silence in the hallways and sidewalks when we passed. Once the closest of friends, we had turned into strangers from petty actions wielding deeply transparent realities.

Insecurity can be a well, and deception weaves a tangled web. Even the most attractive, coveted, and well-connected people harbor envy and crave attention. We all crave love and acceptance. It's a craving that name-brands, labels, make-up, and plastic surgery cannot satisfy. All the parties, trips, and fun-girl adventures would never have filled the void.

Sis,

I would have helped you through it had you not been so determined to bring me down a notch.

I used to miss my girl until I spotted the familiar web spun on someone else years after that incident. At that point, I was too grateful that I chose to distance myself from you even after reconciliation.

Nowadays, I wonder if you ever learned to stand in the strength of your beauty and confidence, or are you still living the façade of appearances as you tear down the trust of others? I wonder, and somehow, I realize I just may never know.

—I Wish Things Could Have Stayed the Same

Doing This Dirty Laundry

To My Sister,

Let me start off by apologizing. Unbeknownst to you, I've ached about this situation for so many years, too many years. It has hurt me watching you live through the pain and abuse you suffered. It has hurt me more than you will ever know, yet it has done more than that. Your pain, and mine, has also hurt us, sister.

Because I've never said anything, you don't know how much I love you. Because you never said anything, I don't know how much the silence ruined us. Even though I cannot rewrite the many years of absence, I can address our deep hurt by telling you what I've learned from you.

Dear Sister,

I've learned so much from you based on the pain you had to endure. I've learned more from your pain than I've learned from your passions—and you've had SO much pain.

One of my deepest pains has been watching you, silently, for all these years as you've encountered and triumphed through your love. Love has hurt you on so many occasions, yet you often try again. All in all, I CANNOT relate, yet the situation is one with which we are ALL very closely acquainted—consciously or otherwise—domestic violence!

It pains me when I hear that women around me are experiencing this issue. By my own count, I have five sisters who have experienced domestic violence at the hands of a boyfriend or husband—three according to their own admission. By my count, I have two brothers who have participated in domestically violent acts—one according to his own admission. HOW DOES ONE RESPOND TO SUCH NEWS?!

1. Engages:

When I was alerted to the first instance of domestic violence, I spoke up. I told others who were around at the time: family. Overall Outcome? Nothing. Nothing changed. I was in college. It was my first year away from home, the same year my granddad passed, and the year my nephew was born. This was already too much. After a while, with no help, support, or even understanding, explanation, or communication from anyone else, responses two and three (below) came quickly into play.

2. Internalizes Feelings

Later in life, more details of the same situation were presented to me. Little did I know, something I brushed off as a one-time occurrence OR the "lie" that it was made out to be was actually a regular pattern within this relationship! I was D E V A S T A T E D, to say the least. It was (un)believable! What was I to do?! The first time I alerted someone, nothing was done. What was the point anyway? By this time, these people were practically married.

3. Gets Numb, Unknowingly

For years, I put my true feelings on the back burner (and I am continuing to, #GloryBE!). Feigned ignorance is a coping mechanism you would think I have mastered by now. To some extent, I have, but with this type of "unlearning" comes the uncanny ability to make myself emotionally unavailable to friends and loved ones who are most in need. In other words, am I really coping? Nah. Not at all. I have simply removed it from my consciousness and pretend like the reality doesn't exist. I do as the Romans do—as the black families do—don't EVER discuss anything that NEEDS to be discussed.

My Sister,

I have shared with only a few of my sisters how I truly feel about what they endure(d). As I reflect now, I realize that the people around those who suffer any type of abuse suffer too. Sometimes, the suffering is based on the lost relationship or losing the ability to relate, which is often most hindering of all. What do you say to a sister experiencing what you can't even imagine? How do you connect with her without exposing her most profound shame, guilt, and regret? How can I love my sisters through their challenges without loving them so much that I try to be a savior? Because when I find out that I can't save any woman from her love, I go on through life in a way that means I now have a hard time loving too.

I struggle with my love, my love, and I am sorry.

I am so sorry for what you have had to endure.

All that you have suffered, I have suffered too.

I miss you.

—Your Awfully Candid Sister

Things
I Never Said

Things I Never Said

BIG SISTERS,

Relationally, I am wealthy. I have a very close-knit family, great friends, those who love me, and those whom I love. I'm blessed to have people who walk with me through every phase of my life. But there is one relationship I desire that I haven't found yet. To be 35 and never married with no prospect in sight or never having had children makes me self-reflect more than anything. No one has come to me and said, "I want to bet it all on you." I've had the occasional date but nothing solid for many years now. It has left me in an interesting place, or should I say an exhausted place?

God has blessed me with much, like a home, a car, promotions, bonuses, etc. Most people would look at me and say, "She has it all," and I am grateful for what I have. This is, by no means, a griping session. However, this is my reality, and with all the people God has surrounded me with, I am still lonely.

I don't share this with people, and I don't say it often. Actually, I've hidden it well. I've always been able to fill my life with other concerns, keeping busy, but it's finally coming to a head. I don't always know what to do with the feelings of not feeling like I'm enough. I know that I am genuinely loved and appreciated. I have people who I love, appreciate, and enjoy having in my corner. To know that someone is rooting for me and concerned about my wellbeing is amazing.

However, there is a part of me that feels I'm still missing something and, for the life of me, I don't know what to do to make that door spring open and allow all the love I still have left to give to be released. I've tried focusing on all the other kinds of love God has surrounded me with. I never want to come off as selfish, like I expect God to give me everything I ask for. I know that even if He doesn't, He still loves me and trusts me; what I'm asking for could just not be on God's time. Maybe there are other things God wants me to complete or other tasks. He would prefer I focus on other completions before that chapter of my life unfolds. I can say the waiting process can do a lot to your self-esteem, honestly.

I know people who have been married several times, but I've never been chosen. I often wonder why that is: what is it about me that isn't enough? Is it me? Is it not me? The older I get, the more frustrated that I have become with not having the answer. Having had several terrible relationships and being cheated on or lied to has been my cup to drink from. Yet I still try to do it right: be the person that a man would be proud to call his.

Let me tell you: doing it right doesn't make a man choose you. No matter how much I cry about it or pray about it, the process will not speed up because I am in an uncomfortable season. The truth is I am enough. I am worthy. And until my King comes, I will continue to do the necessary work within.

LOVE,
Your Baby Sister

The Standard 1.0

Hey Sis,

Today, you missed a meeting because you were on the phone with me, catching up on what was going on in our worlds. The funny thing is, you are the one that is always on point with everything. I was truly surprised when that happened. I know that was a big deal, and you will probably put yourself on punishment for that.

I have watched you sacrifice year after year after year for your family and for your personal goals. I have often said, "You are doing too much" or "Slow down." And you would say, "No, I'm not doing enough."

If I am honest, I thought at times that your process was so selfish and unfair. Over time, I was able to better understand where you were coming from. Once I saw all the responsibilities in your lap, I understood why you had to take the stance you took. Most people cannot handle the amount you have sacrificed, but I have also seen it bring you to a level of success that cannot be discounted.

At times, it made me wonder if I was able to sit in the same arenas as you. You would then begin to tell me all the things you saw in me. You would speak to my strengths and never allowed me to downplay any portion of my story. You helped me to realize I had way more to offer than I was giving myself credit for.

When I think of sacrifice, I think of you. I saw you battle many things over the last few years; some things were harder to watch than others. You are the one who was willing to work 20 hours a day so you could build an empire for your family. There was no limit to your giving when anyone would ask. You have often had to step in to save your family, near and far. I have watched you sacrifice yourself over and over for so many people around you. Your selfless acts were inspirational, but they were also daunting to watch. You just go, go, go, and you don't complain because... well, that's just who you were.

One day, I found out something happened, and you were again put in a position to sacrifice your career for your family. Without hesitation, I saw you give it all up without a second thought. I said to myself, "Wow! If they can't see her love for them now, they never will." And, as I had hoped, the person you gave it all up for actually showed up and showed out for you when it was time to celebrate you.

My Sister:

I write you this letter to say that I honor your sacrifice. The sacrifice that was once intimidating to me is now my point of reference when I think about the amount of mental strength it takes to be great.

You are my sister that I never knew I needed until I needed you. You are a profound influence on my life, and I pray God allows us to be here for each other forever.

You Are the Standard for Greatness; Never Waiver.

—With God, It Always Works Out

Dear Sacrificial Sister

Dear Sacrificial Sister,

Going, Going, Giving, Giving…so many sacrifices. Truth is, I am tired! But I often say, "Lord, use me for your purpose." Could this be the purpose, really, if I feel so depleted at times?

The purpose isn't always pursuit: it's sacrificial. That's been my life for some time now, but my sacrificial investments have been stretched recently.

I am thankful for this journey. However, I must say that I'm exhausted. I embrace that a part of my human existence as a woman gives me multi-tasking creativity. Thank God for that! It has been my balance beam in my recent commitments. Being a wife, mother, daughter, aunt, friend, disciple, ministry leader, business owner, and author are just a few of the roles I am assigned to carry out in this season of my life. There is a measure of sacrifice required for each role with its different expectations. No matter what—or who—I am committed to, I am determined to give my best self regardless of the role.

I must admit, though, that there are times when I feel inadequate, indecisive, and inflicted. This isn't because of incompetence or lack of motivation; it is simply a result of sacrificial stretch. Lord, help me to see the harvest of my sacrificial seeds in so many areas and the lives of others. I don't do anything unless I feel a deep calling or passion for seeding my time, talents, or resources.

There is a special little person in my life that has pressed me to levels of sacrifice I NEVER thought I had in me. His entrance into my life over one year ago has been exhausting but exhilarating! I am committed to nurture, provide, and pour my heart into the safety and success of this little boy. Yikes! What have I done? Lord, was this you? Although this was initially my husband's choice, I quickly partnered with his desire in what I now believe is the will of God for us and the child.

I haven't had to nurture a child hands-on in over 15 years. I wish my husband and I had sought more counsel before embarking on this journey. We didn't know it would cost us at the levels it has. We didn't know that the attachments and attacks would be as great as they are. We didn't realize the adjustments our life would undergo.

But I do know that we\ are also honored to have been available to sacrifice for someone so innocent and inspiring. I often say, "As much as he needed us. We needed him!" I'm discovering that while most days I am tired due to the demands of the season, the reward is so much greater. Today, I am learning to balance it all and view the sacrifice as a blessing, not a burden. I am learning to breathe, relax, and rest. This keeps me in a position to care compassionately, serve sacrificially, and love unconditionally. I have learned that for me to be helpful, I need to be healthy. I'm affirmed that the sacrifices are worth it, and—many times—they are a necessity for a woman like me! It's a part of my makeup to contribute so others can be better.

I must remember to take care of myself so I can be an impactful and positive contributor to all areas that require my sacrificial stretch!

—Willing, Giving, Loving Sister of Sacrifice

I Wish You Would Have Told Me About You

GOD MOMMY,

I wish you would have told me.

I wish you would have told me of all the pain you felt in every relationship you had. I know we didn't have that much time together, and I know we still don't, but…

I wish you would have told me.

I wish you would have told me about all of the things in you that I wanted to see and the things in you that I actually saw and how they spoke truth to the things you never showed.

You never let us know how much he was harming you, how much he was hurting you, how much he was abusing you, how much he caused you to struggle with who you are as a woman. You never let us know about how much he needed you—so much so that you couldn't be what you needed for yourself.

You never let us know that this man's connection with you was so strong that it killed the lifeblood in you. At first, I thought I didn't understand it, but I guess I do because I've seen it happen in myself. There have been times where I have been so entranced by such a man, but why does it happen? Why do we allow it to happen? Why does it happen so much? Because of all that men steal from us, we then steal our shared experiences from women who need these stories. Why are we so ashamed of the lives we're living?

Why is it that—even in our most authentic, honest, open, and trusting relationships—we still put on as if "it's all good," when really, it's not? Life kicks our BUTTS, and that's one thing, but when these men kick our butts, we kick each other's butts! We suffer in silence, even though we see each other walking, talking, living, loving, breathing, and yet we're still NOT RELATING.

I can't relate to what you don't tell me.

I can't relate to what you don't let me in on.

I can't relate because the other side of this is that women regularly anticipate the hate and judgment of other women—even those whom we call sisters. This happens so much so that we then become islands to ourselves. We become idols to ourselves. We say, "I don't want you to judge me, so I'm going to suffer in silence. I'm going to kill myself—softly—because I don't believe you—another woman—can help me to heal myself."

That's what we say to one another.

And so, the day you told me your husband cheated—and kept cheating, and cheating, and cheating—I was hurt. And I was hurt just as much for me as I was hurt for you. I hurt because I wondered, "How did I miss it? How did I miss this?" You needed help I couldn't provide through your walking in graceful silence. I was hurt because you needed something in me that I should have seen. And because I'm a praying woman, I wish I could have prayed my way into your heart. I wish I could have prayed my way into your pain. I wish I could have prayed my way into your own prayers. But I couldn't.

Not without you letting me know. Not without God letting me.

You sat in it by yourself, and I'm sure many more people knew, and I'm sure they love you just as much as I do, but I feel like I'm lacking in some ways now. I feel like I'm lacking because I did not pay enough attention.

I blame myself for much of what you've suffered. I know that's arrogant of me, and I know that's pretty selfish because I'm thinking about me instead of putting this energy into thinking about you, but that's just where we are.

We have our stories, and we have each other, but if we don't share our stories with each other, then what do we really have?

I'm finding out so much about the women around me these days, and I feel like I'm too old to not have known these things sooner. Because of what I didn't know about you, I am threatened to confront some of my own issues.

I wish you would have told me about you. Because if you had told me about you, it would have been a great help to me.

> I Love You, God Mommy, and I Miss You.
> I'm so glad I chose you.

—May You Now Live the Life You Never Dreamed You Could Have

Deal with It OR It Will Deal with You

YOUNGER ME,

Now that I am much older, I understand the wisdom of the proverb that says a whorish man or woman reduces you to a crust of bread and preys upon your precious life. How I wish you could have understood the beauty of the fruit you carry much sooner than later.

Inspirational, vibrant, beautiful you: there is no joy to be found in him, nor him, or him, or any of them! Deny them the places of your deepest vulnerabilities. You open yourself repeatedly for withdrawals while never making deposits. Girlfriend, please protect the sacred spaces because they take, and you give, with no regard for the negative balance.

YOUNGER ME,

What you are seeking is what they can never give, and it costs you far too much. Your dignity has left you. The momentary soothing is no match for the betrayal of your soul, the abuse of your body, or infertility that's awaiting you from scarred tissue and infected tubes that you cannot yet see. Your confidence wanes with each failed transaction, so slow your roll. Better yet, stop altogether, and get to know you.

The fiery passion that you have is not for many; only one deserves the honor and privilege of entrance into sacred spaces—inner chambers. You have not met him yet. It is going to be a while before you do, so settle down. Stop consenting to be the faithful, trustworthy confidant turned temporary lover until the fleeting attention of an untamed, undisciplined, unsubmitted soul finally slows down to seek comfort in another, like you.

YOUNGER ME,

What you sincerely long for is affirmation and acceptance from someone who sees your flaws without exposing them, knows your weaknesses without exploiting them; someone who acknowledges your gifts and calls forth their various expressions; and someone who loves you for who you are, not for what you do. That is what you seek, but sex will not help you find it. The responsibility is yours to block the entrance of selfish intruders who cannot heal the secrecy of your woundedness because they too are wounded. I have some pointers for you if you will receive them:

- Your past is not your present unless you make it.
- Some friendships were never to become any more than that.
- Real friends care about your well-being.
- Physical beauty, though desirable, is superficial; develop your inner spaces.
- There is a God-only part of you that's off-limits, and there, God alone can dwell, heal, and restore. Get in touch with her.
- Evaluate your motives until you learn to stand in the strength of your choices.
- It's okay to say no, and sometimes, it's necessary.
- You can work a fierce stiletto, and that's okay, even while doing Kingdom business.
- Learn to love and discover yourself by discovering the Creator and lover of your soul. Now that's some completely inexhaustible, unconditional love with no boundaries that always gives more than it takes. Invest there.
- Making love is not the same as sex.

- Keep on dancing even when you must change partners.
- Save more, spend less.
- Learn to embrace failures as learning experiences.

Younger Me,

That is my advice to you because I see you struggling to believe the words you use to motivate others. My heart breaks when I see yours in shambles because you gave to another what you should not have given.

Release the shame. You will overcome these seasons of betrayal, self-inflicted wounds, and wounds with trusted friends who are on the same journey.

The time is now to deal with it. If you don't, it will deal with you.

—Older Me, with Much Advice for My Younger Self

Why Not the Good?

HEY SISTER GIRLFRIEND! MY GIRL!

That is how we used to greet each other for years, Sis. I remember those days fondly. I remember the countless days when we spent hours on the phone talking about where we had come from and all of the things we used to do and even the people we used to love. I remember those times I could talk with you about what was going on in my life, and it was as if I were recounting the same details of yours. I remember the times when we were always not far behind one another: when someone saw me, they knew you weren't far behind. We were great friends, sharing our troubles and what brought us the most joy in our childhood. We were committed to praying for one another and being able to share in each other's lives without fear of judgment or shame. It was refreshing to speak freely on whatever we needed advice about or could not reveal to anyone else. I appreciated that. I miss it too.

But let me tell you, even though I miss those times, what I do not miss is looking back and thinking of the crucial occasions you strategically chose to skip out. Even though I can remember all of our most intimate conversations as friends, I cannot recall one time you were there when things were going well for me. When I was stuck in patterns of dysfunctional, self-destructive, disrespectful behaviors, you were there, even facilitating it at times. You were there when all I could think of was all of the wrongs I had done, all of the mistakes I had made. You were there when all I could see were my failures before me.

But as things I had been dreaming about were coming to fruition, you became absent.

Suddenly, you were too tired or too busy. You were too preoccupied with too much to do. What does that mean about our friendship? Does it mean that I was blindly codependent? Does it tell me that you love me, but it reminds you that you are at a standstill?

I went back and forth in my mind many times about it: "Certainly, it's just me being too sensitive." But when I look at my life, there have been too many moments you refused to share in. It puzzled me why you would choose those moments of fulfillment to be absent. It wasn't just moments that made me happy, but you missed moments of divinely ordained purpose—times when I was at my strongest or taking a significant step forward.

So yeah, I miss our conversations. I miss our time. I miss the beautiful relationship we had; we were friends—sister girls. But I'm struggling to let you go because I need someone who will walk with me. Friends celebrate the highs with each other as much as they provide during the lows.

Sometimes the answer we seek comes in a question: Do you condemn me when I'm wrong but applaud my dysfunction? So maybe the truth I need to realize is that in my brokenness, I was complicit in my dysfunction because I had someone who would join me there and co-sign my foolishness.

Do I still have issues? Of course! We all do. But these days, I'm not asking anybody to co-sign my foolishness. I want people to help empower me. I want people to encourage me to live beneath the blessings designed for me. I want people to help me lean into who I am so I can grow into all I ever hope to and am created to be, all that I'm supposed to be. That is what I desire and want for all of my sisters: someone who pushes them forward, gives them a hand up when they are falling, doesn't kick them when they're down, or remind them that they aren't as high up as they hoped they'd be.

So, I guess this is my final goodbye. I'm no longer grieving the loss of you. I am simply celebrating what was and being open to what could possibly be.

If we ever have the conversation we need to—perhaps when we are both in different places, different spaces—these are the things I would say.

—Missing You, but Not Missing My Moments

Dear Munchkin

Dear Trinity,

I can't believe you will be eleven this year. Wow! It was only yesterday you said your first word and took your first step. I have been blessed to be there for many of your firsts. It has truly been my honor to watch you grow, to watch you learn, and to watch you love. You are truly one special little munchkin.

Your wit and smarts are unmatched. I tell your mom that you get your creative side from me. You most definitely got your sassiness and diva style from her. There are so many people who love you and want to see you blossom. You are like my little celebrity munchkin that everyone thinks they know.

It's funny when people ask about you. I love hearing stories about how people have seen you grow over the years. They always ask me how you are and ask me how you have grown. They always say, "How's your munchkin?" You'll always be my munchkin; I hope you know that. It is my prayer that you always know how much I love you. It is my hope that you always feel love and know God's true blessings throughout your life.

When I met you, you were seven months old. The first time we met, you sized me up as if to see if I was worthy of your precious love. You reached out to me and laid your head on my shoulder. From that moment, our hearts became connected, and no matter where this life takes you or I, I will always be your TT.

Dear Trinity,

It's so hard to believe that you are growing up right in front of my eyes. In my mind, you are still the stone-faced chocolate-covered munchkin drop that God knew I needed. I know that you will offer this world so much, and I have no doubt in my mind that the masses will know your name.

You bring so much joy and so much love. And you've done so much of that in such a short amount of time. It is my prayer that you always remember your shine. It is my prayer that you remember who you are and remember whose you are. This life that God has granted you has already been aligned with purpose. The coolest stuff happens at your age; I know you feel that. I know you know you are the smartest chocolate munchkin drop in the whole wide world. Always show that. Always be you. Always speak your truth. Always remind yourself you are beautiful, and you have purpose, and you matter.

I am blessed to witness your growth. One day, I'll tell you how much your coming into my life meant, how much I needed it. God knew exactly when it was time to have you in my life. He knew that I would need you. He knew that I would need an angel to not only watch over me but help me grow. Thank you for loving me and thank you for allowing me to be a part of your life.

Love,
Tee-Tee

September 1st

SEPTEMBER 1ST:

The day we got married.

The day that comes and goes like it holds no weight.

I guess, at this point, it really doesn't matter anymore. Not to say that you never mattered—I just have moved on. I've grown beyond the person I was when I married you: insecure and looking to you for more love than you could give at that time. I came across a recorded interview we did a few years ago. I started to listen, but I deleted it before I had a chance to torture myself with memories.

At one point, I never saw a life without you. At one time, I forced myself to fit into your life, knowing I just did not belong. Whose idea was that anyway? LOL! To get married? I think if we had stayed friends, marriage could have been an adventure we would've looked forward to… maybe. I'm sure you and I both agree it was rushed and should not have happened.

Our marriage, short-lived as it was, taught me a lot about myself. To be honest, when I read your text, "I don't want to be married anymore," I was crushed but also relieved. I felt hurt, embarrassed, stupid, humiliated, betrayed, abandoned, and every other word you can think of that translates into disappointment. I was disappointed in myself for not being the person you wanted me to be. I was disappointed in you for not giving me the chance to love you. I was disappointed in myself for making such a stupid decision.

In hindsight, I don't feel those things anymore, and I definitely don't blame you for what happened between us. It's weird being around you now though; I can't even remember the feeling I once had. I don't see the same person. That in no way is any slight to you. I just know now that we had our moment.

We had a few good times together. I guess for a while, I hoped I could love you through whatever pain you weren't acknowledging. I felt like I could love you hard enough that you would soften, at least a little.

I laugh when I think about how much my friends hated you. But maybe it wasn't hate—maybe they just didn't understand what the hell I was doing or why. I think they just relegated my actions to a midlife crisis. Either way, it didn't matter what they thought or said because I loved you.

Above all, I have no regrets, and my prayer is that every now and then, you smile when you think of me. I certainly do when I think of you.

ALWAYS, IN LIGHT AND IN LOVE,
Your First

No Peace

White Privilege

To:	White Women Colleagues
From:	Me
Re:	Consistent Use of White Privilege

Although this is not a letter, it is official internal business regarding your chronic practice of white privilege. Let this memo serve to address your blatant disregard for a fair and equitable workplace. You have consistently ignored the time and energy your colleagues of color have invested in creating a community built on mutual respect and honoring diversity. This commitment has been repeatedly breached by you, and I will be making some immediate changes to protect my very being and hold you accountable for your actions.

* I will no longer let you speak for me—or other people of color—because you assume you know what is best for us.
* Offering me up as collateral damage will no longer be tolerated.
* When you assume you can use people of color as deflectors when your bottom line and comfort is threatened, you will be called into account.
* Going forward, I will not accept your accolades for making a heroic sacrifice to save you and other white women when I never volunteered to accept the mission.
* I will no longer stand silent behind you, smiling at your imaginary press conference, as you announce your decision to the world—a decision that involves me throwing myself on the

ticking time bomb to save you and your plan, a plan which you have no intentions on sharing.

You have benefited from institutional racism and white privilege since birth, and I have been adversely affected by it every day since my birth. We are contemporaries—yes—and it is quite clear to me that it is politically correct for you to denounce these constructs. However, it is even more apparent that you have absolutely no desire to dismantle institutional racism. Because of this, I will no longer consider your tears, your apologies, or your linguistical slip-ups as you pitifully excuse yourself for not knowing better.

You and I were both raised in the South, so I know you understand the saying, "Every tub must sit on its own bottom." And—at this point—you must finally stand on yours. I am not responsible for educating you about race or how to treat others. White is not always right, nor are you the center of the universe that must be consulted by the rest of humanity. You are at the point of no return, and you have some choices to make.

You are very savvy when it comes to women's rights and holding men accountable for their aggressive and egregious treatment and actions toward women. In the short 60 years since the women's movement, you expect men to get it and get in line. You don't bend or take any lame excuses.

It has been 401 years since the arrival of the first enslaved Africans here and 169 years since Sojourner Truth had this conversation with white women. So, if you are tired of having the conversation with men, you can certainly conclude this conversation is a done deal.

You have thirty days to correct your actions.

This is your last warning.

Your next infraction will be met with appropriate action.

--Tired *Black Woman Who is One Infraction Away from Being Angry*

Choose Life

Sis,

I have wanted to ask what I can do to help you. How can I help you to unpack the suitcase, take off the badge of your trauma, and choose to live? Sometimes life has dealt us a hand we feel we cannot or should not have to play. Countless hours of conversations with friends and private wailing sessions have you weary of talking. Somehow, you have silently but resolutely resigned yourself to defeat and eventual demise. You choose self-degradation, despair, fear of the future, waiting, taunting, and self-inflicted mental paralysis to torment and torture yourself. Hopelessness breeds helplessness in a cynical unjust cycle due to trauma from your past that haunts your present. I know: from the perspective of the shattered heart and battered soul, the world looks different. Diagnoses and inner demons tend to have that effect.

This is not, and never would be, an attempt to trivialize the magnitude of the daily pain you experience—for these are pains that I do not know. However, if I were able, I would take it from you and destroy its residue to erase your memory of its cruelty and unyielding attack. While this is not in my power to do, may I ask for permission to walk alongside you in the wake of personal tragedy? Provide a listening ear or maybe a shoulder to cry on if you need it? No talking or interrogation required. Although I do not have intimate knowledge of your suffering, I pray for your care. I cover you with the same type of graciousness I readily receive each day. Every sister needs that.

BELOVED,

I aspire to remind you of the twinkle in the eye of others that you inspire. I long to introduce you to the fearfully, wonderfully, meticulously, perfectly, and purposefully crafted young woman in your mirror who makes the sun shine brighter when she smiles. Is there no way to usher you to acceptance of life's journey as worth the effort? What if we do it together? Choosing life and checking in.

Can I reacquaint you with the strength of your advocacy, power of your voice, high heels, healthy living, laughter, and "light of the world" life? What about days gone by when social media comparisons were non-existent? Lattes and lazy days were welcomed, along with finding a great eatery or channeling your inner author, poet, or dancer. We cannot choose the hand we are dealt. However, we can still choose what we do with that hand.

I implore you: Choose to live for the rest of the time that you have life. Resolve to receive the gift of life with joy. Take the little and make it more. Share the felt expressions of your experiences so that the world can hear. If you did, it could ignite the flames for you to discuss pain that others are ashamed to discuss, and maybe, you might be encouraged to see the value of your contribution. In that way, you and others will live supported, appreciated, and no longer suffering in the deafening isolation of silence.

I know it will be hard to consider choosing life, but know that I love you, my sister.

—Your Dear and Beloved Friend of God

Daughter of a Black Sheep

Hey Sis,

Do you remember when you were in the chorus? It still makes me laugh to remember how excited you were when you made the ensemble team.

Remember how good it felt to be a part of something? That would be your chance to get out of the shadows. They would see you then. You did your part. You learned the songs. You sang in front of the class. Well, you held a note in front of the class. You had the permission slip signed, and the only thing to do next was to get the uniform. No big deal: all you had to do was tell your guardians, and they would make it happen. I mean, they are supposed to support your dreams, right? You followed the rules and didn't get into much trouble except for your flippant tongue. So, surely, they would allow you to sing in the chorus.

Do you remember when they said they were not going to buy the dress? Maybe that's why you wear so many dresses now. Do you remember how sad you were and how upset you were? In your mind, it just didn't make sense. You saw them allow others to participate in band. And *that* came with fees, but for you, the fee was too great. That was the first time you felt different or less than. It was almost as if they were quietly putting you back in your place, making you feel like you didn't matter or you weren't enough.

Being overlooked or rejected became commonplace for you. As they teased you about appearance, your hair, your family, and so many things other things, they were subconsciously trying to break down your self-esteem. But life continued to throw you curveballs, and you consistently jumped right out of the way. You were built to adapt and overcome adversity.

Just wait until you blossom; they will all eat those words.

SISTER,

The wounds inflicted on you during your childhood can last for a long time, but they do not have to define who you will become. Those wounds make your skin tough, yet I pray you never internalize the thoughts of others. I pray you never allow their thoughts to bring you to doubt yourself.

Sister, you are phenomenal, and your strength will be the guide to your purpose. The way they made you feel is not indicative of who you were, who you are, or who you will become. My sister, we all need the rejection, for it what helps us to grow. You see, they didn't know it, but they were setting you up to be able to stand strong in the face of a NO. Now, you take those no's, you *devour* them, and you move on.

The pain you felt as a child—being rejected or overlooked—was real. That same pain is also what taught you how not to treat your own children or others you care for. If I could have given you something for you to hold on to that would remind you of who you were as a child, it would be the words of Maya Angelou's beautiful poem, Phenomenal Woman. Through those words and these, begin to see yourself as the phenomenal woman that you truly are.

—A Phenomenal Woman, That's YOU

Menopause

Dear Menopause,

I have become a different person since you took over my body, my LIFE! I was once full of energy and over-the-top optimism. I was happy and adventuresome. Now, I constantly struggle in my body and in my spirit just to be as normal as I can. I have learned the hard way that in this 21st century, no one cares about women who suffer from you. I know you already know this, but it sure surprised me that other women just don't care. I once thought they just didn't know what to say or do. I mean, I can understand that it's painful to witness a woman enduring an episode of heat, sweat, or losing focus because of the many stages of you.

Women giggle when I fan myself because I'm burning from the inside out. They ask dumb questions about why this is happening while offering inappropriate advice about how I can be less conspicuous because my fanning is distracting. I'm angry at their silence when a man announces that I'm having a 'hot flash' or 'personal summer.' Just to be clear, you are anything but a 'flash,' and it's neither personal nor seasonal. You show up applying extreme heat from my waist to the top of my head every 30-40 minutes. It lasts a full 10 minutes, which leaves sweat running down my back, underneath my clothes. You apply the heat until I can hardly breathe. I am discouraged by the many female physicians, specialists, and websites that suggest and say outright that you might be uncomfortable and sometimes painful. Yet, the experts try to soften this blow by saying it's a normal and manageable part of aging. Manageable?! Really? Men are never asked to live with or manage any phase of aging. Little blue pills were invented to fix men. Now, they expect women to "manage" their gifts of low sex drive, depression, and insomnia by entertaining the men who partake in the pill. *sigh*

Menopause,

You are neither cute nor amusing. But you can still help me out! Talk to the women who can't relate, the ones who think this can be fixed by drinking Fiji water or eating tofu from Tibet. Tell them that taking the age-old Lady Pinkham remedy for 'female complaints' or drinking ginseng tea while standing on one foot that they can keep their suggestions to themselves. They are not helpful, especially not when I'm in the middle of an episode. Frankly, it's downright hurtful!

Sisters Who Don't Care,

Maybe, you just don't know what to do or say, but let me speak directly to you: Your silence is killing your grandmothers, mothers, sisters, partners, sisters-in-love, daughters, daughters-in-love, nieces, granddaughters, and girls yet unborn. Menopause has preyed on women for centuries, virtually unchanged and unchecked. I'm sure Lydia Pinkham (1819-1883), a feminist who gave it her best shot with *Lady Pinkham* an herbal remedy, would be outraged that her product is still sold today using a slightly modified formula. There has been no cutting-edge advancement since then because it is a women's problem. No one cares, not even women. What a pity and a shame.

> *I write these words hoping you'd be drawn to feel my pain,*
> *and if you can't feel for me, then feel for you,*
> *and let's do something about it!*
> *You might not be the one with a cure, and that is okay,*
> *but let's give voice to something we've silently lived with for*
> *far too long. Silence says you don't care.*
> *Let's vow to be silent no more.*

—*A Sister Who Is Tired of Suffering Alone*

Sister, You Hate Me

To My Biological Sister,

One of the worst days of my life was probably the day I found out you hate me.

You hate me!

Nothing in my mind can get me to understand how we got to this point.

All I ever wanted was to be your sister, your joy. All I ever wanted was to be your friend. All I ever wanted was to protect you, yet...

You hate me.

So much of our relationship has been unspoken social cues we have come to experience as a lifelong lack of relationship. At the same time, I believe we simply tolerate each other. I love you, but I must say that "tolerate" is what I have to do in order to keep my eyes on you. And I keep my eyes on you, not because I'm threatened by you or shocked by the *latest* news I get about how much you don't like me; I keep my eyes on you because I love you. Despite all my love—much of which has caused the huge chasm in our relationship today—you hate me.

I wonder...

What in the world have I done to cause you to hate me? What did I really do? As far as I know, I've done nothing, and I bet if I asked you, you don't even know why.

You hate me for free.

And you think that's okay while not understanding how much your hate for me impedes the progress we can make and the progress everything attached to us can make.

SISTER,

Whether you like me or not, hate is a bit too strong for what we have here. I feel like in order to hate me, you had to love me at some point, and I don't see too many elements of our life where you have shown a deep love for me. That's been unfortunate because I once thought everything that came from you was absolutely sincere. I have now come to find out that it was all a lie. All of your praise: it was a lie. All of your pride in me: it was a lie. All of your support of me: it was a lie because every few years, it comes back to me again—through people we know and love, and trust—that you hate me.
HATE!
I can't believe it.
And imagine me, again, just trying to be everything you knew and everything you loved and everything that could represent you. I mean, I literally wanted to be like you, and you're over there just hating me for nothing I've done to you...to YOU! But because of what you believe I have done to you, apparently, I've caused you a lot of pain for reasons I don't know. And for that, I sincerely apologize.

SISTER,

I apologize for every time I didn't understand you enough to go the extra mile and talk to you about things, things that I did not cause. I apologize for every time that—instead of just listening to you—I felt I needed to defend myself. Because of my defending myself, perhaps you don't know who you are to me. Perhaps—because of my defending myself—I've told you about too much of who I am. As a result, I guess I have not seen enough of you. I apologize that—in my trying to be all that you needed and all that you wanted and all that I could be to make you proud—I lost myself by trying to find myself in you. I apologize for losing so much sight of my own identity that I have created a wedge between us that has caused us an inability to relate to each other.

It's disturbing, ya know. It's disturbing that it looks good: it looks like all fun and games. We put on a show. I mean, I thought what I was doing was authentic and true, but you hate me.

Hate.

Me.

sigh

I guess I have to let it go.

I'm too old at this point to keep on holding on to the sister I never had and a sister I will never have. I don't even know if my heart is open enough at this moment to tell you, "When you are ready, I'll be here." I just don't know. I don't know if it's safe for me to say that because I don't know if I can tolerate, yet again, another acknowledgment that you hate me.

And maybe you always have.

—Endured Entirely Too Much of Your Hate-Inflicted Pain

We Will Be Okay

ANOTHER MESSAGE TO MYSELF:

I found a Tweet from a girl named Ro that really speaks to me:

> *"I'll say it again...*
> *I used to think communication was key until I realized comprehension is. You can communicate all you want with someone, but if they don't understand you, it's silent chaos."*

I would say that I am very experienced in relationships because I have experienced some of the most insane situations. Throughout every relationship, I always believed that the relationship didn't work because I was misunderstood. "Nobody gets me," I said. "Why is it that we aren't on the same page?" or "Why can't we see eye to eye?"

In most cases, communication was the root of my relationship problems. I have been in heterosexual and homosexual relationships—and outside of trust—communication is crucial in every relationship you have.

To communicate with me, let me know what you want, when you want it, and how you want it. If you feel some type of way, express yourself when you feel comfortable, but AT LEAST communicate that you aren't ready to talk. Be transparent. Even if you THINK there is something I should know, why not just tell me? Communication goes a long way.

I still believe that communication is key, but over the years, I have found it is much deeper than that. Like Twitter girl, Ro, said, "You can communicate all you want, but if they don't understand you, it's silent chaos." So again, please don't let me just talk and talk, especially when you don't want to listen, and my words are going in one ear and out the other. That's when my blood begins to boil, and I feel misunderstood. Ask questions if you don't understand. Unless one person simply does not care to listen, there shouldn't be any reason why relationships go in communication circles; both parties should listen to comprehend. My partner's response to my comments lets me know whether they understood anything I said.

So...

How did I get here?

Honestly, I would have never thought I would be back together with you. When we were first together, we were young, but now we are growing every day to become the best versions of ourselves. You have become more assertive, and I have become more confident, but we still have much work to do. You still don't know when to implement boundaries that will help you balance and respect other relationships in your life. And because of that, we struggle.

I have been telling you for months now that you must create balance in your life using boundaries. Although you've listened and mentioned how much you understand, months later, you still demonstrate passiveness. Anyone can interrupt us. You seem to put anyone above me or our relationship.

How did we get here?

Do you even really want this? I refuse, I refuse, I refuse to allow myself to go down this road again where I feel less appreciated every day. I hope and pray that you eventually understand me.

Although I speak to you in this letter, there is also another message for myself.

I have to remind myself when enough is enough.

Listening to comprehend and not just listening to react is one of OUR keys to a healthy relationship. We are not in a relationship by ourselves—it takes two to tango. Your issue may be learning to actually listen and understand while I continue to battle with maintaining confidence. Yes, I have become more confident, but I still have a dark side to me. Battling low self-esteem, depression, and suicide, I periodically fall back into the trap at times. There are moments when I feel like I am so misunderstood that it hinders my confidence. It makes me question my purpose in this relationship and on Earth—why am I here? I sometimes feel like I have this heavy weight on my back, and nobody has the answer or solution to lighten it. I often joke and say that if I had a therapist, they would probably give me back. All jokes have some truth.

It's true: I do feel like I am too much. Even though you continue to tell me time after time that I am enough, that I am beautiful and loved, I can't completely shake that feeling of inadequacy. I can only imagine how frustrating it may be on your end to have a girlfriend who constantly talks down on herself. I know it can be a turn-off. I pray that one day I can fully accept who God has created me to be. I am fearfully and wonderfully made. I have to learn to love me enough for both of us.

—We Will Be Okay

Unspoken

Hey!

I want to apologize for all of the times I have hurt you and projected my shortcomings onto you. I apologize for creating challenges between us due to a lack of accountability or my inability to directly communicate my feelings. I want you to know it always has been my mission to love, support, and protect you.

I am addicted to your mind and afflicted by your presence. I thought I was protecting you when I denied myself. It took me years to figure out that denying myself did not serve either of us.

I apologize that my love for you felt like a burden more than a blessing. I've never liked confrontation and have always aimed to make things right. However, I don't know how; I have not done well handling challenges or personal conversations.

In my life, I don't fight for myself or the opportunities I want. However, you taught me how to love myself.

**Learning how to love myself
and all my imperfections
was challenging but necessary.**

In times past, I let promising opportunities dissolve. In my efforts to not cause anyone strife or pain, I sometimes end up doing exactly that.

I miss you and know that we could never be together because of our worlds and how life has happened.

Unspoken thoughts and feelings still flood my mind concerning you and us. I know your focus lies in other areas, and that's okay. To have known you in this short space of my life was necessary. I'm learning to embrace the moments we've shared. I appreciate you more and more as I go through life. Every lesson learned, every challenging conversation, every tear was all worth it because *you are* worth it, and *I am* worth it.

It would always excite me and upset me how you noticed everything. I wish I could be as in tune with you.

Know that I am extremely grateful for our time together. Know that I am so proud of your progress and respect who you are and who you are becoming. You made me BELIEVE IT!

What is It, you ask? LIFE!

You made me believe life was worth living in color and OUT LOUD!

> THANK YOU!
> Unspoken

RECLAIMING WHAT WAS LOST

Dear Forgiven and Free

DEAR FORGIVEN AND FREE,

Whom the Son sets FREE is FREE indeed.

Today, I am thankful for the forgiveness and freedom that exist in my life. Not many years ago, I experienced my first encounter with a lack of forgiveness. I have always been the one to NEVER hold grudges. Always compassionate, gracious, forgiving, and understanding. Everyone has bad days and bad moments, right? So, I tend to give people the benefit of the doubt with a dab of extra grace.

Well, I thought I was walking in forgiveness and being a great role model. Lord was I wrong! I didn't even realize it until years after the blow that I was harboring certain feelings in my heart toward a particular individual. They hurt me so bad that I felt abandoned. The moment our relationship experienced some form of normalcy and restoration, I thought those feelings were gone. The feelings were just suppressed. I was saying I had forgiven them, but I hadn't.

Growing up as an only child to both my parents, I was extremely blessed. My grandparents on both sides spoiled me, and so did my aunts and uncles. I was the oldest grandchild on both sides of the family, so that came with perks. Life was great! I never went without; my family was functional, and I didn't have any voids. Until BOOM!!!

My parents are no longer together. Now, I am in the middle. Initially, there was no real effect on me, but as time went on, I got older, and my parents moved on. Things were a little different. Now, I loved my family, but I didn't understand why we were in that space. Why did Mom have a man that wasn't Daddy? Why did Daddy have a new woman that wasn't Mom? It just didn't seem fair. God, why is my family broken? Why are my parents not happy together? It seems they are happier without each other.

I was young, hurting, confused, and upset, not knowing until I was older that I had not forgiven my parents for their separation. Why didn't someone explain this to me? Why didn't they ask me how I felt? Didn't anyone care about my feelings? Maybe they didn't think it mattered to me. I was just a little girl. But it did matter.

Years later, I became separated from Dad for several years. This resulted in him missing some very important moments in my life: graduation, my wedding day, significant accomplishments, and other major moments. When the time came for us to reunite, I was so wounded but longed for the connection so bad until I didn't avail myself of the restoration I needed. I needed to forgive him for the early years of separation because I realized I had piled in the early years of disappointment and abandonment.

When we reconnected, it was a conversation that revealed my heart. Thank God for maturity and honesty; I shared my heart with Dad, and soon, my disappointment and hurt tied to their separation. I also expressed my confusion about my parents moving on with their lives. As happy as they were after parting ways, I just didn't understand.

Today, I am grateful that my parents moved on. I now know that their connection was for a particular time and purpose: ME! I now know that they didn't know how to express what they were working through. Neither did they know the impact their splitting up had on me as a little girl.

Although I was always the understanding and forgiving one, I am grateful that I had my encounter with not being able to forgive. It was painful but liberating for the way I manage relationships: it revealed the difficulty of trusting new seasons when you haven't dealt with seasons of the past. I am encouraged today because had it not been for the separation, I wouldn't value forgiveness and the purity of stable, successful relationships today.

—Forgiving, and Free

Get Back Up

Sister,

I just wanted to drop you a couple of lines to let you know that I know that you are hurting. You have fallen pretty hard, and I can see you are at a very low point in life. But I want to encourage you not to stay there. I know you have fallen far from grace. I know that you made a wrong choice, or in your words, another bad choice and another lousy choice, and another wrong choice. But Sis—we have all made bad, lousy, wrong choices on more than one occasion. We have cycles and seasons that play out in our lives. That is a part of our growing process. Be willing to extend grace to yourself—the same grace that you are always ready to extend to others. Redirect that same encouragement you use to help others recognize that these occasions are opportunities to learn and grow. I pray you can receive and embrace this for yourself.

Forgive Yourself, Sis...

...the same way you've been able to walk through the process of forgiving those who caused you harm, those who shut you out or those who have not been in your corner. Be willing to forgive yourself the way you were ready to fight through forgiving those you love and others for whom you care. Dealing compassionately with friends who betrayed you or friends who were absent when you needed them is your way. So, I encourage you to be a friend to yourself. Forgive yourself for not stepping up and being fully present in your life; forgive yourself for not being able to say no when you should have said no.

You'll continue to beat yourself up if you do not forgive yourself. Don't' stay in this lowly state of self-condemnation by depriving yourself of walking in the joy and strength of who you are.

Let Yourself Off The Hook, Sis.

Yes, you did it; you made a choice. Yes, you've made bad decisions, but don't look over your life and count all your past missteps against yourself. Don't count all the wrong decisions you made and all of the things you decided to do that you should not have done. The more you do that, the deeper you sink. Yes, some of those choices and decisions have had lasting consequences, but they've also all taught you some precious lessons.

Sis,

Let the lessons speak louder than the pain; let the life lessons and the wisdom that comes from failing forward help you begin to embrace better choices. Learn the lessons, embrace the lessons, and let go of the guilt; let go of the shame, let go of the grudge you hold against yourself, and turn the grace that you give to others around to face you. Do this so you can love yourself more fully because when you're free to love yourself, you're free to love others.

Give yourself time. Give yourself the necessary space for growth. Give yourself what you need so you can embrace a different thought process. Define the words that affirm who you are and speak those words of life to yourself about yourself: hang them on the wall; put them on note cards and carry them with you in your purse; post some of them in your car; type them on your phone. Do whatever it is that you have to do so you carry a constant remember of who you were created to be and all of the beautiful things about you because you are fearfully and wonderfully made, and what you did does not change that.

Sis,

Stop wearing the guilt. Remove the shame. Take it off and forgive yourself for being human.

I FORGIVE YOU.
And I pray that you will forgive you, too.

—Always Standing Behind You, Always Standing Strong

Free to Love

Hey Sis,

I want you to know it's okay to love again.

SIS,

Know that love is a very peculiar thing, and there is no rhyme or reason to it. You have to feel it from within and experience it in its fullness.

I know you feel like you will never love again. I know you are feeling numb. I know that you can't seem to find your way through the walls that you have built to protect yourself, but it is okay to come out of hiding. It is okay to let your guard down a little. I mean, you do not want to be alone forever, do you? Which past issue was it that held you back from trying again today?

- The married man:

    You say: "Ohh, sis! I love him so much. He is good to me. He takes care of me. He makes me feel safe. He is nice to my children. He makes sure the little things are taken care of. I do not get to spend a lot of time with him. Well, you know, because he has his own family that comes before me. Yeah, it's a hard pill to swallow, but you know I love him, so it's worth it to me."

I say: Hey sis, love him, but walk away!!! I know it's easier said than done, but look in the mirror and tell yourself, "I'm worth more than this!"

Somewhere along the way, you lost your identity fooling with this man. The married man treats you like an option because he has to make sure his main priority—HOME—is taken care of first. Sis, it is a hard truth. You will be the one left holding the bag... GET OUT!!!

* The abusive man:

I know. I see you in all your designer and smelling sooo good, but did you know not even the most expensive MAC makeup can hide tracks of your tears?

Hey sis, I see you crying out for help, but you do not know where to turn. You are worth the fight to get away. He will not stop hurting you until he breaks you. You have to stand up for yourself right now. Yes sis, I know it's not physical!!! But I gotta tell you: the mental and verbal abuse is worse because it goes unnoticed. I SEE YOU THOUGH!!! In every word he uses to demean you, I see you in every chance he takes to make you seem incompetent. I see you every time he makes you feel unpretty. I see you every time he makes you feel unworthy. I see you every time he makes you feel dumb.

Sis, I know it takes a lot to muster up the courage to leave an abusive relationship because it comes with some great perks. But I also know that you are EVERYTHING THAT HE SAYS YOU ARE NOT!!! I need you to believe it for yourself. If it were not so, he would not be so hell-bent on breaking you down.

WAKE UP, SIS!
THERE IS HELP AND HEALING FOR YOU!!!

* The dead man:

This man hurts the most. He loved you, and you loved him. I see the sadness in your eyes. I see you overcompensate for your loss. Sis, I know the pain you feel can never be dismissed. The hurt makes you feel like you do not want to love again; you don't want to be vulnerable again. You do not want to get too close because you don't want to lose another man.

The loss of this man triggers memories of losing all the other people you have ever loved. I know you are afraid and lonely, but you are allowed to love again. You must first live again.

Give yourself permission to keep living.

You can't let your love die with your loved one. It's gonna be hard, Sis, but I promise to be with you. I promise to help you get through the frogs until your heart finds its new mate.

You deserve to love and be loved again. You owe life to yourself, unapologetically. God gave you another chance; take advantage of it. I love you, and I support you. I pray you ask God to give you your love back. Ask God to give you the desire to love and be loved again. There is no guilt or shame in wanting and needing a companion. Woman was not meant to be alone, my SISTER—that means YOU![7]

—Be Free to Love!!!

---

[7] Biblical Reference to Genesis 2:18 which says, "Then the LORD God said, "It is not good for the man to live alone. I will make a suitable companion to help him. *(GNT)*"

You Are Not Alone!

Hey Girl!

I hope this letter finds you well!

I'm writing to let you know that it's okay to give your pain a voice and a name. I want to acknowledge all the hurt, pain, trauma, and disappointment you've experienced.

Recently, I learned of several traumatic events that occurred during your childhood. At the moment, the reveal of such things sat with me for weeks. My heart ached to know that you had to live through those experiences alone. My mind could not grasp how someone could do those things to a woman they love and cherish—a woman who was but a child. Although you've lived through those life experiences, be reminded of how brave you are.

To decide to rid yourself of shame and break the silence was the first step toward healing. Having sought help through therapy and counseling to sort through your emotional stress and anger is another milestone. Permitting yourself to confront your opponent(s) gracefully, or kicking and screaming, takes courage.

Know that you aren't in this alone. Know that you weren't alone in this fight! I don't know why bad things happen to good sisters, but I know that you didn't deserve such horrific things happening to you. You are a survivor; you are a conqueror. Every day that you wake up, suit up, and choose to live because you are a WINNER! I am your family, a friend, and a confidant.

As you heal through this pain, remember to celebrate all that you ARE and all that you EMBODY.

I want you to know that I am forever grateful for your friendship. One of your greatest attributes is your energy and smile. When you walk into any space, your energy shines. Continue to allow your LIGHT to shine through dark moments, dark memories, and shady people.

Forgive your parents for their lack of parenting. Show them grace, understanding their lifestyles collided during darkness, yet they were able to birth a ray of sunshine: YOU! Many times, our parents are only able to share our well of ups and downs.

Forgive yourself for all the decisions you'll make for the sake of providing and protecting yourself. Life's not about being right; it's about exploring.

Forgive yourself for falling in and out of love. Take the time to reflect on what you need; what does love look like to you in action? Strive to exude the love of your creator and share it with others.

Don't forget to thank yourself for all the times you'll CHOOSE You! Choosing you never gets old, and in return, you give the world your best!

Lastly, your strength lives within; remember you possess all the sources you need to BE you! Nobody will ever do you better! Be Free from your past and your pains and live your life without REGRET!

You are not alone.

We are in this thing called life TOGETHER!

—Your Sister, Your Confidant, Your Friend

you

Hey Girl!

If you could describe the way you view yourself, what would you say? I know it is hard to describe the positive or find the *right* words to say. Take some time to look at yourself. Take time to explore your being, to help cultivate who you are becoming. Learning and loving who you are and who you will evolve into is a journey you travel as long as you are alive.

First, I want to tell you that you are beautiful the way you are. Enjoy the evolution of your body. Be aware of the changes you'll experience as a result of age, life experiences, and while building relationships with yourself and others. Always remember that your body is a temple: sacred, pure, and powerful. Feed your temple, temper your breathing, and nurture your mind with positive thinking. Through prayer and meditation, become one with your body—practice adorning your body and stimulating your mind. As your body and mind connect, it will provide mental stability that will birth a *knowing* within.

Baby girl,

Your smile is contagious, your eyes brown and beautiful. Your skin a perfect mixture between almond butter and brown sugar. Your legs are long and robust for walking the long roads you travel in life;

you are set to change the world through acts of love. Your arms are strong and warm, used to embrace yourself and others during challenging times. Your breasts are small and petite, yet always front and center. Small doesn't mean less powerful or less beautiful. Love them; they won't get bigger! Embrace your scars; they tell stories of triumphs. The dark spots are shadows of what was but remember, they give space for the new. Love your mole; it's a beauty statement. The curls and coils of your hair embody grace and will be a trend that never goes out of style. Love the width in your hips; someday, you will give birth to a movement of ideas and children. Always keep the light glowing in your eyes. Never dress to impress others, but still dress to adorn and impress *yourself*. Learn to live life in color; this provides an avenue to be creative and open. Colors are an expression of your heart and innovative ideas. Leave the black and white to your pen selection. Living in color will help you be more open to change and exploration. Remember, your scars tell a story that reminds you of how far you've come.

Pamper yourself:
plan a spa day of meditation and prayer.

Then, light a candle, and play your favorite playlist: music will help you stay centered and mentally balanced. Make *you* a priority so—as you navigate through life—you'll become more aware.

Be accountable to your own needs and desires,
and learn to boldly articulate them.

—Me

Baby Girl, It's Time to Listen (to Yourself)

TO MY BEAUTIFUL, FATIGUED SELF:

I wish you would have said all the things you did not say. For years, you've baggage that was not yours—these weights, these pains, and these concerns are not yours to bear. You should have left them where you found them: with the person who has caused you so much agony. And it's not just one person. It's person after person after person. *And anotha one!*

For a lifetime, you've carried the bags of others. You've made the pain of others be your pain because you felt that bearing their burdens would express your love. You felt that keeping silent when you should have spoken out was the way they could best know you love them. Instead of getting angry when you could have, you said nothing. Instead of verbalizing your responses, you did nothing. And in years and years of doing nothing, you've broken your back to please others who—come to find out — just will not be pleased anyway.

You see, it's not the silence, my love. It's not the wisdom of it all. It's not the road less traveled that has been a burden for you. It has been not saying your peace when your silence has caused people to grossly misunderstand and abuse you and your love.

Your love is a love that is too strong to be shattered. It is too reinforced by your faith to be broken. Yet still, you have borne love through bearing burdens that are not yours to carry in the first place. And because you once wore your love like a slave in the chains of other people's pains, you now have a hard time branching out and finding true love or even sustainable friendship.

They could have appreciated your wisdom enough to say, "Hey, what do you think? Really? Don't tell me what I want to hear. Tell me what I need to hear." And you—because of your big voice—have decided not to share it with your people, or with the world. Your silence has not only allowed many relationships to stay broken, but your silence has now broken you.

They don't even want to hear how you feel about your own pains. Because of it, you've not been able to be true. You've not been able to hold your weight in spaces that don't welcome you because you don't welcome their drama.

Baby Girl,

You've gotta find yourself again. You've gotta dig yourself up through all the wreckage. Life, love, and an attempt at silent liberty have caused you to create an inauthentic sense of your reality. You must create a reality that is not built on relationships you silence while walking alongside others who would rather not listen. And it is okay to find yourself in a new space. It is okay to look in the mirror and say, "Hey, I don't like the self I have been, and I need to be a *new* me *for* me." It's okay to do all of that. What is not okay is to hold on to things you should let go of right now. So, I am asking my dear if you would listen. Just listen this one time, even if you never listened to me before.

Baby Girl: Let It Go!

Let go of everyone's judgment. Let go of everyone's assessment of you. Let go of everyone's need of you because their need for you is not healthy. It's not healing you in the places where you are broken. Their need for you is not listening to you. Listening to yourself allows you to open your mouth, open your heart, and share everything you need to share. So, open your heart and shed all the tears you need to cry.

You need to listen. Listen to your pain. Listen to your temperature. Listen to your motion. Listen to your heartache. Listen to your headache, and if others won't listen to you, Baby Girl, it's time you start listening to yourself.

—A Young, Anxious Girl Growing into a Bold, Beautiful Woman

The Girl Misses Her Daddy

To All My Sisters, All the Daughters,

There's a girl out there who's daddy is missing. He's visible in her life, not quite the absent father, yet...

He's still...

Missing.

It's not his presence that has departed, but it is him. She misses... him. Her. The girl misses her daddy.

Daddies wear such a big hat in the role of any daughter. Yet sometimes we assume that mothers play the biggest role in the development of a daughter. Sometimes, as women, we need to bear our all—tell the stories of how important fathers are in our lives. For when we don't, we limit the affirmation of the black male and do not readily acknowledge the players who are missing from the development of the black female.

We accept the absence of these daddy-daughter roles and force girls to become women before time. We force marriages that cannot develop because of a lacking model in the history of the young girl. Therefore, grown women are young girls who marry boys. Seeing as though this missing daddy impacts the young man just as well as the young woman, when daddies are not exemplified as both head and hero, we break down the family unit of all black persons and somehow end up being confused as to why women walk around as we do. Many black women share a similar problem: the girl misses her daddy.

In our present time, if we do not reclaim what was once the father as the head and the daughter as his love alive, we miss out on the opportunity to groom women in ways that will change lives and entire communities through many generations of black folk.

This is a call to each of us as women to reclaim what is ours through reclaiming our men. For when just one man is lost to this wanton world of wickedness, so too are we lost as women. When we cannot stand behind our men, we also cannot stand together with one another. Now, I'm not saying that our men are perfect, but if we can learn to perfect our relationships, and once again put our men as the head, we then will understand that to submit and subject ourselves to the leadership of our black brothers and black fathers is not to lose anything of our nature and essence as powerful soul sisters. Instead, to affirm the leading nature of our males by restoring his placement and pride, we also reclaim his innate ability to nurture us through love, protection, and care. To restore the placement of the daddy is to gain everything, for when just one daughter misses her daddy, we miss the reclaiming of an identity where there was clan and there was king.

Daughters,

I'm calling on you to reclaim. Reclaim your position by putting your dads back on the throne. That means putting pride aside, putting aside count of his indecencies and no longer judging your father according to discrepancies. Judge your father according to his rightful headship. Without learning to look at your dad in a way that admires him, you no longer relish and respect the posture of being adored by a man in charge. For it is adoration that a daughter should seek from her daddy because if a daughter is adored by her daddy, not one man in this world can tear down her identity, nor will her daddy miss out on what matters most in his identity: birthing love that only births more love.

**Though you miss your daddy,
be the love that births more love.**

—A Girl Who Misses Her Daddy Too

Sistah Mamas: I Wonder Why

SISTAH,

I pray you can perceive the motive behind this story.

Have you ever loved someone so much you wanted to give them what they did not have the capacity to receive?

She did.

She loved him with all her mind, heart, soul, and strength; she was all in. They were in love—both fine, chocolate, sexy people. Oh! Maybe you don't like that kind of talk. Just know that they were a handsome couple.

Both were gainfully employed, working toward a better future. His smile and playful banter piqued her interest, but it was the sweet talk, smooth lines, and his being eight years her senior that sealed the deal. He had seen the world in military service, rocked the world of many long before he crossed her path. And told everybody she knew, "She's going to be my wife." Their relationship appeared to be the kind dreams were made of: fun-filled times of dancing the night away, road-trips, wining, and dining.

It was all great but not destined to last for too long. Broken promises and large blocks of unaccounted for time soon proved to be evidence of the lie he had been living for quite a while: he had a wife on the other side of town.

I've always wanted to ask her, "Sis, why did you stay? What about him made you wait to fix him and lose *you* in the process?" I couldn't because I was simply a young girl eavesdropping, as it were. I listened in on the stories of grown women. They were quick to let you know you had not lived enough life to understand what makes a woman endure such emotional manipulation, such torture of the soul. I wondered in silence if she could not recognize the way her heart's beauty shone through the false tough exterior. "Don't you know that he is not even all that? Nope, not worth having to fight or run from every other Friday or Saturday night when she had to flee from his drug and alcohol-infused fits of rage. Black-eyes, busted lips, bloodied noses, bruised bodies were not unusual amidst good company, magic cornrowing fingers, healing rituals, and the best-fried chicken ever. I want to ask her why she stayed or ask another just like her, "Why don't you just put him out?" But I cannot because she is no longer alive, and neither is the other one or the other one.

These women loved others so much they forgot to love themselves properly, even unto death.

Sistah Mamas:

I was hoping you could live the wisdom you give others and smell the fragrant aroma that surrounds you. I just wanted to see you receive these blessings in return, but now you are gone. The Sistah Mamas that are left are now weary in well-doing and feeble in their steps. I wonder if they have ever known a lover who was entirely honest and completely free to love them back. They cared so deeply for others. As surrogate mothers, neighborhood grandmothers, community leaders, and evangelists, they fed the hungry. They washed the clothes, soles, and souls of others, all the while unwittingly ignoring their own.

Dear Sistah Mamas,

I pray you can perceive the motive behind this story.
I pray you can care for you just as much as you care for me.

—Child of a Sistah Mama

Black Lesbian Loves

Dear Black Lesbian Woman,

Here we are in a world that sometimes makes us feel like we don't belong here. We battle racism, but we also battle homophobia within our own community. Where do we feel safe? Constantly trying to prove our worth and purpose for our existence in every way.

What words can I say to bring you comfort?

What I want you to know first is that you are not alone. I know what that feels like. To feel alone. To feel like no one understands you. To feel like no one understands the things that trigger you emotionally. I am you. I've been you my entire life. Sometimes you wonder who will fight for and stand for you. Who will give voice to all that you are feeling? I don't know everything there is to know in this life, but I do know that everything you are feeling does get better. Even if it doesn't feel like it ever will get better, keep living. Keep pushing. Tell your story authentically and truthfully.

Take it one day at a time. Heck! Take it one hour at a time if you must; just push through. You are stronger than you realize and more powerful than you feel. Please try not to put more pressure on yourself than needed.

How others feel about you matters not. What matters most is how you feel about yourself. Take some time to fall in love with you, with all of you. The good, the bad, the parts you hide from the rest of the world. Fall deeply in love with that person in every way possible. What you will find is that the love you have focused on yourself will begin to show outwardly. It will begin to seep into your friendships, your intimate relationships, your family. Your spirit will begin to reject anything and anyone who mean you no good.

In no way do I want you to believe that this will be an easy process. It won't. It will probably be the hardest thing you have ever done or will do in this life. It will be worth it though; you will be worth it. Every tear that falls, every scream, every desire to punch walls—or people, LOL—don't do that, will all be worth it.

I am not the most religious person in the world, but I do believe that whatever higher power you believe in has already given you everything that you need to fulfill your purpose. *Your* purpose! That is all this life is about, finding and fulfilling purpose, beloved. You are worthy of this life. From the moment that you were thought of to this very moment, even if you feel helpless, you are worthy and worth it.

Whatever your purpose is, I believe that you will find it. I believe that if you just keep pushing and pressing forward one more day, it will be revealed to you. Push through this day, then the next, then the one after that and the one after that. Focus on giving yourself the love that you are seeking from others and watch how sufficient God's grace becomes for you.

Choose to Live, Beloved; All Will Be Well.

IN LIGHT,
Your Reflection

MOTHERS AND THEIR CHILDREN

What Happened to Our Voice

Dear Mom,

Once, in middle school, I was tasked with a homework assignment to write about my mother and complete a family tree. I was super excited to get started and had lots of plans for this assignment to be perfect. However, it was at that moment I realized I did not know intricate details about your past. I discovered that you'd never share the parts of your life that caused you pain or power. You never shared your childhood dreams or hobbies. Years later, this list of things you kept to yourself began to grow. You never shared matters of the heart or lessons about parenting, dating, marriage, sex, or sexuality.

Back then, your voice was a silence that lingered over our home—a forbidden discussion not to be challenged, but it prompted questions that still weigh heavy in my mind. Your voice spoke volumes of pain that I assumed crippled your ability to speak.

And I've often wondered what made you so quiet. What experiences were you hiding because of shame or guilt? What stories must be told to free you and me? I always wished you knew that sharing would bring our hearts closer together and heal us both.

When you were diagnosed with cancer, you never spoke about it—your decision to keep quiet translated into me learning to live life in secret. When I found out you were sick, my heart ached for two reasons: you didn't mention it so that we could support you through it, and I was scared I would lose you. I couldn't imagine you leaving this earth without any explanation of what happened and why. We should have been allowed an opportunity to openly share as a family how your diagnosis affected us.

Once you started the recovery phase, I was instructed on the dos and don'ts of managing my feelings and responses. I wasn't given the freedom to express myself during this time. Somehow, through your lack of sharing, I assumed a role of uncertainty. I felt an unworthiness of not truly knowing you in our relationship as mother and daughter.

Eventually, I even adapted the stigma that silence was golden, yet what I came to know is that silence is darkness—crippling and ugly to live with. There were moments when you embraced me with hugs, and somehow, I then felt your heartbeat for me.

Mom, if I could offer any strength to you from daughter to mother, woman to woman, here is what I propose:

Start confronting your past today so you can be at peace. Perhaps this will help you redefine your passions in life. Your history shouldn't have to be a silent memory because that makes it your present and your future.

MOTHER,
You are beautiful!

— Your Little Girl Who Has Finally Found Her Voice

Understanding

Hey Mama,

You did what you thought was best.

You were twenty-four with four kids and didn't have much help, and here comes this family offering you the help you need; offering to take on the physical and financial responsibilities; offering help that looked and sounded a lot like freedom. You loved me as your baby, but you knew they could give so much more than you. So, you gave me over to what seemed to be the best option.

I still wonder if this is the outcome you expected. Did you know we would live in what felt like two separate worlds? When you dropped me off, did you ever look back? All these years later, you have all these memories of me; you remember being in places where I've never seen you, but all I remember is your absence. I have seen pictures of me packed and ready to go to see you, but I don't have any memories of going.

It's funny how what helps one person can hurt another. There was a time that your absence was hurtful to me: you gave me up for a better life, but to me, it felt like you didn't want me. I wish you would have called me now and then to remind me that I was yours. Growing up, it was hard trying to remember the sound of your voice and what you looked like. Knowing that you had another baby after me made me feel replaceable. Seeing you show up to sign papers to give me away made me feel unwanted.

Those are the only memories I have of you.

I didn't understand the gravity of your decision until I was a mother myself. When I learned how hard it was to take care of a child, I understood why you sent me away. As a new mom on hard days, I thought several times about being like you. Sending my baby to a family that could just give him what I could not. Then I remembered those nights I spent crying because my family was not like everyone else's. I remembered those crushing reminders of feeling unwanted, and I couldn't bring myself to do that to another person—especially not to the one who was entrusted to my care. So, I tied a knot in my rope and decided to hang on; I wanted to prove to myself that I wasn't like you.

In my quest to be so unlike you, I still didn't turn into the most amazing mom. That's the crazy thing about judgment, I guess. You spend so much time focused on the things about a person you don't want that you tune out the parts of them you should keep. If I had focused on the positive parts of you, I would have seen your selflessness; and I would have done some things differently.

Mama,

I'm not mad anymore; I understand you now, but the hurt places are still healing, so just give me some time. I want to build a future with you because we don't have a past. By learning about you, I hope to better understand me.

—A Girl, Just Working to Understand

Letter to My Mother

Ma!

You're my mother, and yet you call me out of my name. These names aren't even curse words, but you've called me everything but a child of God. There's so much criticism out of your mouth these days, I can't help but wonder how you have felt about me all my life. It's shameful, really, that my own mother cannot speak life into me.

Just recently, I started to have a problem with your verbal abuse. Once I did start, I wondered how long you had been doing this and how long I had been letting you. It seems that your abuse had been happening for so long that it became normal for me, and I just dealt with it.

I dealt with you.

And from the words coming out of your mouth, it seems like you're doing nothing but dealing with me.

But I am your child. I am your daughter.

You're my mother, for heaven's sake!

Why is it that my mother is the last one who says something good to me? If you do say something nice, it's because I've done something that is just outwardly good. I don't understand why you can't say something nice just because—just because I am your daughter and because I mean that much to you or even because you *want* me to mean that much to... well, myself!

What mother does that?

Mothers give their daughters a hard time. I understand that.

Daughters give their mothers a hard time. I understand that too.

Yet, at the same time, I wonder how much of my giving you a hard time is a direct response to you giving me the business every single chance you get. It's quite sickening, if you ask me, quite unnatural for you to be an all-in-all good person and still be the one who doles out my most critical assessments. And they come constantly and unceasingly.

Well, Ma, I had to stop and finally ask myself, "How much of this is really not about me? How much of it is about you?"

Mom,

What about your life has gotten so bad that you have to critique your own daughter? What about your life has been so horrible that you spew nothingness out of your mouth all the time? And thank God I'm an affirmed woman! Thank God I know who I am! If I didn't, I'd be dead waiting for *you* to say something that was going to speak life to *me*.

It's quite apparent that what we have here is a lack of ability to communicate. And if I don't happen to be around you all the time, and if I don't happen to *want* to be around you all the time, you should probably understand. It should be obvious to you why I'm not snuggled up in your arms all the time. I mean, how harmful would it be to me if I did? How tragic would it be to me if I set myself under your criticism constantly? I definitely wouldn't be the woman I am today, even though your abuse is the reason I AM the woman I am today!

What, about your life, makes you talk to me like I'm nothing? You don't understand how important it is for you to say something so good to me that it not only creates my tomorrows, but it directly *pushes* me into beautiful tomorrows.

Mom,

I shouldn't have to find affirmation from anybody outside of you. Every affirmation that comes outside of you should just be a bonus. Why is it that you aren't the one uplifting me? Why is it that you aren't the one that births out of me greatness in understanding that I am the life that came out of you!

Every time your words sting me, every time your words harm me, every time your words infect me, you are bringing death to the very life that you created.

—Your Aching Daughter

I Don't Resent You

Dear Mama,

Though you did not necessarily raise me, I still felt your presence during my childhood. Though you made some bad decisions that cost our time together as mother and daughter, I never stopped loving you. You never told me the full truth. But I learned from my brothers that you endured some dark moments in your life. I wish you had the help you needed. I wish your brothers and sisters knew how to reach you. I wish something clicked back then when you were on drugs. I don't know what life was like for you, but it must have been a painful time for needles to be your go-to.

Learning the details of your past life hurt me a lot; even then, I didn't resent you. I learned that our rat-infested house was filled with needles hidden in the couch and junk everywhere. I would never have thought we lived like that, but I only experience these things through my brother's stories.

But Mama,

Through it all, you are still the greatest mom. You have been through a lot: drugs, domestic violence, and homelessness. You lost all your kids, but you still made your mark in all our lives, one way or another.

I was 26 when I finally found out the impact my father had on the decisions you made in your life. Why didn't you tell me? I did not know my father sold cocaine. I didn't know my father ran an escort service. I didn't know he cheated on you multiple times and hit you. Why didn't you tell me? I made my father out to be an angel when, in reality, he inflicted a lot of pain on you. I never knew about either of your pasts until now.

I guess I'm a lot like you in that way, always seeing the good in people. I appreciate you. I salute you. I don't resent you. I don't resent my father either. Although I should, my heart just won't let me.

After moving in with my aunt and cousins because daddy went to prison and it became tough for you to take care of me, I didn't want anything more than for my family to be back together again. I hated living with them, and your lies to get me there really frustrated our relationship. I apologize, though, for the talking back and disrespect, but I just want you to know the real reason why we temporarily fell apart. Now, we are like two peas in a pod—best friends—like mother, like daughter.

Thank you, Mama.

You never gave up on me. You continued to do whatever you could to be in my life. Although, you weren't present physically or financially, you showered me with the love only a mother can give, and I am forever grateful. I am so thankful that God has His hand on you. I am so grateful for you being able to turn your life over to Christ and quit smoking. I am so thankful that you have grown so much mentally.

Thank you for never giving up.

Unlike most of our family members, especially my brothers, I don't resent you. It's like people wanted me to hate you for how things happened, but I could never. I love you. The only thing I will say is, continue to be YOU. Don't let the negativity from any of our family members get you down.

THANK YOU FOR BEING MY MOM.
I love you forever and always.

The Rose of Sharon

THE ROSE OF SHARON:

Mother—my rock, my everything. Honestly, the way I am feeling these days, I smile with even the slightest thought of you. I think about you in every move I make. I think about all the ways I can repay you for everything you've done for me, knowing that it will never equate to what you've provided. I often think to myself, "I'm going to give that lady everything she's ever dreamed of." You deserve it.

I know we don't talk about your strength often, but you are something else! I can't imagine the hurt you felt and still feel from Daddy leaving or what it took to keep going despite everything he did and didn't do. But despite it all, you always made sure I had what I needed. When our water heater broke, we would boil water in the biggest pot we had and pour it into the tub. When we needed to keep the refrigerator cold, we would freeze gallons of water—2-3 at a time—and put them in the fridge until it was time to do it all over again. When our stove went out, we cooked everything in the microwave, and then when you went out, you brought a mini burner from school—one of the ones you used for your science class—I don't think I ever told you this, but I hated science. Of course, though, I thought it was cool to have a science teacher as a mom—you're like my own personal Bill Nye.

In hindsight and with distance, I realize that we did go without. But it was only material things. We always had each other. You had me when my dad decided not to be a father. I had you when grandma passed, and you didn't know how you would go on, let alone if you even wanted to. No matter how many times I thought you were too hard on me, you always went above and beyond to make sure I always had what I needed, even if it wasn't always what I wanted. The foundation you laid for me has kept me cared for to this day.

There are times I can't even begin to explain to you the things I've been through that I know would break your heart. What I want you to know, what I hope to show you with this life you gave me, is that everything you've instilled in me will keep me going and always does. I am strong because you are, and you always have been. So, even when life throws me curveballs, you showed me who and *whose* I was.

Everything I am is because of you, and—for as long as I have breath in my body—I will shout it from the mountain tops and let the whole world know that you are my momma, and I will always be your Tee-Tee.

Love,
Tee-Tee

Tears for You

Dear Mama,

As a young girl, maybe I didn't favor you too much. I mean, I favored you, yet we had—and still have—so much in common that it is probably these striking similarities that make us feel like we're worlds apart.

Mom,

You have always been—and still are—the best thing that ever happened to me. Although we still find ourselves entangled in our seeming disdain for one another, we have a connection that can never be broken. At times, that connection seems built on strife and division, but at its core, I believe we know that we love each other more than we can sometimes bear.

Mother,

As I grow older, I find that my love for you intensifies every time I see women who are tormented within themselves. You see, I appreciate you, mother. Your toughness, firmness, and the traits that tore us apart from physical love or encouraging words are the same things that make me more resilient, more brave, and more willing to try and face the world.

Mom,

I am grateful for the combination of your love and God's love. The grouping of the two in the body that God created for me, coupled with this mind and this resolve, have a predetermined outcome that I still don't fully understand. But I promise you, every day I recognize that the tears I cried as a child based on what I felt was lacking love from you built me into a woman who appreciates all you stood for more than anything else in this world. As a mature woman, I appreciate all you were back then and all you were not. Exposure to your sometimes hurtful mothering allows me to see that although you might not always do what I have wanted you to do, there are very few areas in your pattern where I could ever truly say, "Mama isn't right." I believe it is just as they say it is: Mama is always right. And, Mama, that is the connection that I once missed.

I'm happy that as an adult woman, I found myself back in a place where I can respect and acknowledge who you are. Unfortunately, most of these acknowledgments come as other imperfect mothering is revealed. I've seen mothers who seem to have been a bit more careless with their own daughters. I've seen mothers who might have been a bit more hurtful to their daughters. I've seen mothers who might have been a bit more friendly with their daughters. And the combination of these things makes me more appreciate you, my mother, all the more. You see, we don't always get the mother we want. We may not always get the mother that we feel we deserve, but in my own case especially, I feel we just might get the exact mothers that we need.

It's about time that all the little daughters and big daughters realize that we will not ever have the perfect mother. Every mother will be flawed, but it is our responses to our mothers and their methods coupled with the condition of our lives that gives us the ability to decide how we will respond to the deck we have been given.

Mom,

In my own case, I am grateful for the ability to accept you as you are now. I'm not all the way there yet, but I'm working on it, and I'm grateful for you and your patience with me since my responses to you have not always been favorable. Because I admire you more and more every day, I pray I can accept you completely—preferably sooner than later. I pray I can fully accept all other mothers, too, while understanding that mothering is the hardest thing anyone has ever done in life.

We are hard on our mothers—daughters most especially—yet I know that some of these same mothers will give up on themselves before they ever give up on us. For that, I am grateful.

—I Love You, Mommy!

Healing in the Household

Sisters on the Run

DEAR SISTER,

Today, I thought of you and realized how alone you must feel. For years, I wondered why you were the way you are: so distant and cold. At times, no one would know you exist if they hadn't known us from childhood.

Believe it or not, I love you so much and pray that you are well and in good health as you travel all over the world. I often wonder if you think of me at all. I wonder if you consider me your sister anymore.

We are different in so many ways. I guess we have always been this way. I wonder if you feel the loneliness and isolation like I do. I wonder why you stayed away from family, but I also understand. As I have decided to let everyone live in their own truth because I desire the same grace, but I believe it may be a disservice to us all. Where is the connection? What keeps us together? Where is the sisterly bond? Do you desire to figure it out? Is this just another generational curse that puts one sister against the other? It's such a shame because our mother's branch of the family tree was already so small.

I have seen you deal with so many things, and you always come out unscathed, but I see the pain you carry deep down inside. I have allowed myself to believe it is all too painful for you to come home, which also gives me peace knowing that's the decision you had to make for yourself. I miss you, but I also love you and respect your decision.

In life, we must learn to accept the fate of others. We are not in control of how our lives will turn out. Love never ceases, and the love I have for you will never go away. The blood we share from our mother's womb will always keep us connected in this world. There is no place far enough to outrun love.

My prayer is that GOD will allow reconciliation. My prayer for us both is peace with our past that our futures can once again collide. One day, we will sit and be able to discuss what happened to us. I pray we both will let go of our pride and shame and guilt and be able to freely discuss the things that broke our family. We have always heard the cliché, "Blood is thicker than water." But time has shown me that even blood relationships must be cultivated.

Love does conquer all, but silence builds a bridge that is very hard to travel over. Words unspoken are often the gateway to healing. I pray you know that I love you. More than ever, it is my heart's desire that our children live above the curses that have plagued our family for so many generations. Perhaps even it shall be our children's children who will be the ones to break the curse.

MY sister: may I say that I am so proud of the woman you have become. I am so glad you chose your own path, and you are living life on your own terms.

UNTIL WE MEET AGAIN,
Godspeed.

—Waiting for You to Run Back Home to Me

Pride Over Relationship

DEAR SISTER,

I would like to talk to you about how you make me feel. I often hear things in the wind, and I let them go because of our relationship. But I need you to own up to your stuff; I am actually starting to feel like you don't like me at all.

Yes, I know we are too old to be concerned if someone likes us or not. But you are my family, and I love you. When I hear insults you say or imply about me, it hurts my feelings. The part that hurts the most is that I still can't walk away even though I am feeling dismissed.

I can't deny that the love I have for you is so strong. And If I am honest with you, I really want to walk away, but I can't. I wish there were a magic wand that could erase the hurt and leave all the good times. But life and reality is what it is, and we all know that the wand is but a fairy tale.

I don't know if I hurt you or did something wrong, but I would like to say I'm sorry. See, I am at a point where I can acknowledge that I have a role to play in all things that happen in my life. It doesn't matter if I feel I am right or wrong; there is always something I could have done better. So, I am sorry I let my pride stop me from trying to fix the issue. I chose to let it continue to get out of control.

I am trying to be and do better, so I can be a better example for my children. I hope my apology helps break the generational curse of having to be right and having to be hard.

I have decided I refuse to lose this relationship. People are dying left and right, and I know I pretend to be unbothered, but it bothers me! This lie I tell myself and others haunts me when I see you in pictures or even your name on a text message, but I was giving in to my pride. I was not going to worry about salvaging the relationship anymore, but I was wrong. I couldn't do that. I truly love you, and my love for you won't let me leave you alone.

I am not saying that what happened in the relationship was cool, but I am saying I don't want to fight anymore. I am saying I was hurt, but I am not willing to let the hurt consume me. The growth is in forgiving, and the reconciliation is in the conversation, but the truth will be revealed in the change of behavior.

I pray that one day we will be able to get things back to the way they were. There are certain people that are put on this earth that we are assigned to, and I believe I'm assigned to you. That means I can never walk away, so tell me I suck. Tell me how stupid I am. And then, let's hug it out and move forward in love. True transparency will be the only way we can get through this.

—*I Leave This in My Heart and Hope for the Courage to Walk it Out*

I Am So Sorry, I Forgot

HEY SIS,

Hope you're having a great day. Just wanted to make sure to reach out to you so I could apologize. I'm not sure exactly what happened to make me forget just how amazing you are and what God has bestowed on you: all these gifts and talents.

I cannot quite put my finger on what happened to make me forget that God opens doors no man can shut. I'm not sure what caused me to forget there is a purpose and a plan for your life far greater than any failures, far greater than any of the mistakes. I forgot that the purpose and plan ordained for you before time supersedes anything that you could have ever done. All things have been orchestrated to work together and bring you to that very same expected end. People would be blessed by those gifts, by the great purpose that has been laid out for you.

I'm sorry that I forgot. I'm so sorry you have forgotten. I'm sorry I didn't remind you that everything happens for a reason.

I apologize for not remembering that the work begun in you will be carried to completion. We are all a work in progress: your failures, your faults, even your flows can be divinely woven into the tapestry of your life.

Failure isn't final.

I wish I would have remembered to tell you that.

I forgot to let you know that the life lessons you learn will be invaluable in helping you empower and engage others. Help them receive the message you give because your life has shown itself as tried and true. You know what trouble is; you've had to overcome it many times. So, I encourage you to remember who God is even though somehow, you have forgotten who you are. I encourage you to remember what God says, even though you've told yourself all kinds of things that are contrary to what he has told you. His voice is *the* voice that should speak louder than your feeling, than your pain. God's voice is *the* voice that should be brighter than the dimly lit places in the secrecy of your woundedness.

Please don't permit life to steal your joy. Please don't allow mistakes to cause you to forfeit the beauty and greatness of God's plan for you. Eyes haven't seen—and ears haven't heard—the uniqueness of perspective that can only come from the filter of your specific experience. The world needs your voice.

I apologize that I let you forget. I apologize that I forgot to remember.

Remembering would have spared you the turmoil of listening, so I speak to you those things that already are, although it appears that sometimes they are not. I challenge you to walk in the destiny God has for you. I challenge you to not sit down, to shrink back no longer, to refuse to shrivel up. Do not shut down. Walk bravely and boldly in the face of adversity, in the face of fear, and even in the face of self-doubt. Walk the path that has been laid out for you until you move into the space God has already paved for you.

SISTER,

I pray I never again forget to tell you that you are fearfully and wonderfully made. You are fashioned in God's image—for God's purposes—with works ordained and prepared for you to do in advance. You are the Creator's workmanship: a living, breathing masterpiece.

My prayer is that you never forget. The pain of perpetual isolation and misguided insulation was driven by insecurities and immature emotions left unchecked by others. Your pain results from looking through the lenses of a woman driven by offense rather than her faith. I hope I never forget to remind you again.

> GREATNESS IS IN YOU,
> and greater awaits.
>
> *—I Will Never Again Forget*

Women Who Hate Women

DEAR HEART,

I've seen so much hate in this world, so many women hating women. And the problem is not that women hate other women, but the problem is that women hate themselves. You see, when we don't love ourselves with a good, thick, deep-layered, buttery-flavored, tender love, we simply have no capacity to let that love spill out onto others in ways that cleanse souls. Personally, I'm looking for a soul-cleansing, mind-bending love. No longer can I stand for a back-breaking, tedious, argumentative, and divisive love. I see so much of that, and you must know... I mean, I really see too much of it, and I have repeatedly been forced to realize I have a huge disdain for hate-filled women. Now, I hate to scorn hateful women, but if I don't shun 'em, I might just allow their lacking love for self to press me to shun myself.

Because of whom these abrasive sisters represent—and because of how women treat one another—we all begin to hate parts of ourselves when we witness the hate-filled hearts of other black, and brown, women. We must acknowledge who we represent. We must acknowledge what we represent. What is it about this world that has created this nature? What is it about this world that has created this fierceness? Have we not learned to be bold and courageous without being bitter and crass? Frankly, I tire of fighting with women to show them that I love 'em. I tire of fighting with myself for going back and forth with abrasive women in a battle that already seems lost.

Dear Heart,

I need you to understand that women who are broken create more broken women. Hateful women create more hateful women. And sometimes, we feel guilty and responsible for the problems we witness in our sisters. Then, instead of fixing what we fed, we excuse it away by saying, "Well, she's seen so many things. She's been through so much." Yes! She's been through so many things; all women have, but the question I posed to you today is: Have we loved one another through many things?

As women, we must stop letting bad experiences eat away at our heartstrings because experience does not define us as much as heart does. Experiences can give birth to bloody, bleeding, black hearts, yet if we learn to cope through our hearts' honest emotions, we also learn to spread love in ways that allow us to heal. Once we express our experiences in ways that free us, we find that our hearts can endure the deepest of aches through the darkest of pains. When women hold on to negativity more readily than our ability to love, we allow life's hurdles to control our minds, bodies, and souls. Where, young lady, is the bliss in that? Where is the opportunity to live beyond that? Woe to each of us when we align with negativity and death as if our hearts are not stronger than whatever this hell on Earth will allow.

Dear Heart,

I encourage you to reclaim your heart with a sense of urgency no matter how dead it is, and I understand it could very well be dead. But choose life! Choose to live again. Choose to love again. Choose to breathe again. You do that first by exhaling.

Let go of all the hurt and stop holding your hurt higher than your desire to heal. Stop using past negative experiences to tell the story of your future. When you do that, you explain away your ability to change by making everything—and everybody—else responsible for how your life turned out. If that's the case, if everything outside of you has control over you, you are not truly living anyway; you've already allowed life to win.

Now, of course, I don't want to quit. I simply want you to get to a point where you understand that every day when you open your eyes, you have a new chance, a new opportunity to try love again. I'm not telling you that your experiences weren't worthy reasons to want to quit. Yet I am telling you that—if you can—find it in your heart... find just one little spark, one little spark of tenderness, that allows you to feel alive again. Then, feed that tiny seed with water, with love, and with light. And put yourself in better situations with better people so you can freely live again.

When you expect better for yourself, you can expect better from people. You will find that life provides more opportunities if you just keep pushing forward. If life allowed you to wake up, if God allowed you to breathe again, then I'd say that's worth giving it a shot. Try again, my sister, and I promise you, you will not regret it. Just remember: every day, you must make a choice to live. No matter what happened yesterday and no matter what you anticipate tomorrow, every day and every moment give you a new chance to live.

Make a choice to love.
Make a choice to laugh.

—I am Rooting for You, Dear Heart, and I'll See You on the Journey

Behold, I Will Do a NEW Thing
(God-versations)

Dear Determined Sister

Dear Determined Sister,

Time flies when you are having fun—fulfilling purpose and pursuing destiny! As amazing as my journey is, I have found that I get tired along the way. I've experienced victories, valleys, grief, goodies, challenges, and celebrations! And it's all been worth it.

When I decided to embark upon the pursuit of destiny, I understood that I was in for a marathon, not a sprint. I've had to trust the process and remember that there is an expected end! I had to make up my mind early in the game because quitting is not an option, but completion is the outcome.

Wheeewww!

I'm making it.

I am still in the race. No matter where I am on the journey, I am determined not to end up bruised but better; winning, not worried; strong, and not stressed! I am determined to finish strong!

I am so blessed to have accomplished so much this far, but there is so much more to get done, and I know can finish strong!

Webster defines strong as having great strength, having moral or intellectual power, and being effective or efficient, especially in a specified direction. All of these are very valid; however, in addition to Webster, I have discovered that strong is defined as also defined as having GOD!

Acts 17:28 (GNT) says: "'In him, we live and move and exist." That is strength all in itself. Paul said in II Corinthians 12:10 (*GNT*),

"I am content with weaknesses, insults, hardships, persecutions, and difficulties for Christ's sake. For when I am weak, then I am strong." This expresses a strength that is pressed out of the journey. Finally, God says to Paul in II Corinthians 12:9 (GNT), "'My grace is all you need, for my power is greatest when you are weak.'"

Hallelujah...

This is why I embrace the fact to be strong is to be in GOD! I have had to embrace my weaknesses to see strength manifested in my life! I believe God allows me to finish strong when I tap into the uniqueness of my own humanity, which forces me to rely on the divine to accomplish anything! This is so refreshing and encouraging. I know I don't have to do this on my own. The prescription for my STRONG finish is to take a dose of my own humanity and mix my weaknesses with His POWER and Word and expect to complete my task in victory.

On my journey, I'm employing tools to finish strong:

Stay Submitted: I have discovered that being submitted unto God, aligned with His will, and surrendering to His way will make my journey smoother.

Thrive: Regardless of what I have experienced and what I may have to face. I choose to stay in pursuit and keep thriving! I refuse to get sucked into simply surviving.

Release: I don't hold grudges, grievances, or garbage! I truly believe that the biggest enemy to a strong finish is my inability to release along the way. I can't finish anything if I am too burdened to get in/stay in pursuit.

Obey: Stay in order. Finishing is a by-product of obedience. I'm not threatened by obedience, so I can obey my way into victory.

Non-Negotiables: The only way I will finish is to have a non-negotiable approach. I set standards, maintain standards, and commit to living out my standard!

Grow: As long as I'm in pursuit, I will keep GROWING! Finishing strong is about completion, not finality. I'm on a journey of evolving and becoming! I refuse to stop growing.

I believe I have it in me to accomplish everything in God's creative intent for me. I am excited as I stay in pursuit. I trust that there is an expected end, and I'm destined to finish STRONG!

—*Determined and Making It*

Not What I Had Planned

Sister,

If you had asked my younger self, I would never have been a single mom—that wasn't in the cards for me. All I ever wanted to do was be a wife and mother. I didn't just want a baby: I wanted five. I wanted to be the mom who was always busy with her babies and living her dream. I wanted to balance being a wife, mother, and businesswoman whose family was so rooted in Christ that we were GOALS.

That is what I wanted for my life.

Imagine my disappointment when I was 19 and became a single mom. I still can't remember if my judgment of myself was harsher than the judgment of others. I felt like I had lost my way, so my goals shifted, and I said I wanted to be married before my son turned five. I wanted us to have started our life as a family by the time he started kindergarten.

Well, kindergarten came—and went—and I wasn't even in a relationship. I found myself looking to God like, "Hey, did you forget about me here?! I'm asking you for something!" In my eyes, God didn't budge. Two years later, when I thought I was seeing the end of this side street I had put myself on, I thought God was finally about to do it. I was in a relationship thinking it was headed to that marriage and big family I had been asking for. We were studying the Bible and having deep conversations. This was it, right? This was God about to do what I had been asking Him to do!

So, there I was, sitting at the doctor's, giving him all these updates about my life, and answering all the questions that he had. He ran a few tests, ordered labs, and told me to schedule a follow-up. The follow-up came, and my doctor said everything looked fine, but he wanted to get some ultrasounds done. We scheduled those and another follow-up. Surely, doc was just being cautious because he wanted to make sure that I wouldn't have anything to worry about when God answered my prayers, right?

After the ultrasound, I headed back to the doctor, and he told me what every woman wants to hear. "Everything looks fine." He told me there were a couple of numbers that could be different but nothing that said I wasn't healthy. I was happy. I was excited! "This is going to be the year. God has answered my prayers."

Then, it happened. My doctor said, "I'm concerned. Based on what you're saying, even with these results, you still may not be able to have more children."

He went on to tell me that because everything looked fine, there was really nothing for him to fix. My body just wasn't doing what it needed to do.

I held it together.

I kept a straight face while walking those long hallways to get out of the building. But when I got to my car, I broke. Tears flooded my eyes and ran down my face the way rain cascades down windshields during Florida thunderstorms. I didn't understand why God was punishing me. "I made one mistake, and because of it, you're going to keep me from my dreams?"

I drove home and climbed into bed; I didn't have the energy to give the world anything else that day. I felt like God had turned His back on me.

I tried to stay in bed for the next two days, but life needed me. I had a job, I had a son, and I had responsibilities. I talked *at* God several times, not waiting to hear back from Him. I told Him how I felt, and what I thought He needed to hear. I found myself reminding God how good I was to Him: I was a faithful giver. I evangelized to others. I was a light. I was calling things out to God like I was doing Him a favor. When I finally stopped talking long enough to hear Him, His response was simple: "Be joyful in hope, patient in affliction, faithful in prayer." That simple statement from Romans 12 brought me to my knees.

You see, I heard what the doctor said and forgot *whose* I was. I was so busy reminding God that He hadn't done what I asked Him to do, all the while neglecting what He *had* done. I hadn't mastered parenting my *one* child, so who said I was ready for more? I was asking God to be a genie instead of being who He was: GOD.

Every day isn't easy, and my faith is still growing, but I am exactly what that scripture tells me to be: faithful in prayer.

God produces miracles, so if God decides to change my situation, I know He is able.

I always keep in mind when Habakkuk asked the Lord, "How long shall I ask for help, and you not hear?" The Lord's reply to him is what I'm holding on to: "For I am doing a work in your days that you would not believe if I told you."

—*Still Waiting on the Faithfulness of My Faithful Father, God*

When Has God Failed You?

DEAR 37-YEAR-OLD ME,

So, here you are: 24 years beyond the first thought of suicide; 1 year past your last thought; 20 years beyond your first attempt; 4 years past your last attempt. On this day, I would venture to say that you are beginning to truly understand the magnitude of your being. There's spirituality in it all: the necessary pain, lessons learned, and the knowledge that this carnal existence is a temporary one.

Everything you have been through, good, and bad, has shaped you into the woman you are today. You have so much to do. You have many more lessons to learn. You have more purpose to fulfill. I truly pray you continue to hold onto that. I pray you reflect on the times God came through with every promise He revealed to you.

I pray that—in moments of darkness or in those times you feel alone—you take a moment to breathe and allow yourself to feel whatever it is you may be feeling at that moment. Cry. And release. Let that stuff go. And let it come out of you *completely*. Allow the tears to cradle you to sleep. Take a shower and allow those same tears to evaporate. Breathe. Say a prayer. Smile. Even if you don't feel like it. Allow the curling of your lips to help you remember what it feels like to smile. Let it stay there until your heart is ready to move forward. Play some music: anything inspirational.

You know exactly where to go. You know exactly what to do. Remember that first thought 24 years ago. Remember that last one. Remember that first attempt at 17. Remember that last one at 32.

Look at you, living!
Look at you, defying the odds.

Look at you, remembering who you are: being magical and succeeding past your own limitations and doubts. Love will soon find you, and when it does, it will show you why you had to endure all that you have to become the person you've grown to be.

You are stronger and more powerful than you realize. You are just now beginning to see your magic. Keep hold of that. Stay the course. Take more trips and write. Do everything you've been afraid to do. What do you have to lose? The only battle you are fighting is in your mind. And I know this human thing can get tricky: trying to figure it all out, navigating uncharted seas, and walking alone. But remember that you are never truly alone.

Instructions are written in your DNA: God's only requirement of you is to keep going, keep fighting and keep pushing. Pray more. Stand on faith more. Move more. Take more risks that scare you. Leap and the net will appear, they say. Hasn't He shown you that constantly? Name one time that God wasn't there for you; I'll wait.

Keep going, baby girl.

Remember that God has and always will have your back. God said, "If you will, He will." Let's go!

IN LIGHT,
You

—God Has NEVER Failed

No Limits Sister

Dear No-Limits Sister,

> *"To him who by means of his power working in us is able to do so much more than we can ever ask for, or even think of."*
>
> *Ephesians 3:20 GNT*

★ **We Have: A Limited Humanity**

The very nature of our humanity poses the potential of limits. The Bible tells us that "Man that is born of a woman is of few days and full of trouble" (*Job 14:1 KJV*). That verse alone suggests limits. In several accounts, the Bible reminds us that our humanity has perimeters and a set capacity.

The Bible reminds us that this body is decaying daily, which further confirms that our humanity is limited. Our mere humanity exposes limits. Limits are a reality for all who are on this Christian journey. It is a privilege to encounter challenges on this walk as a reminder that regardless of our limitations, there are no limitations in God!

★ **We Serve: A Limitless God**

God is amazing! He's all-knowing, all-powerful, and everywhere! There is no failure in Him! He reigns over everything. As believers who are human yet spiritual, we have to have confidence that is beyond us!

There's NO LIMITATION IN GOD! I don't know about you, but that TRULY excites me. It is inspiring and encouraging!

The Bible reminds me, "I alone know the plans I have for you, plans to bring you prosperity and not disaster, plans to bring about the future you hope for" (*JER 29:11 GNT*).

Whatever you are hoping for, you can still experience it, regardless of your limitations!
Keep pressing and hoping for it. It can happen for you because our God is Limitless!

★ My Limitations

I'm a very active, vibrant, and destiny-driven young lady. By that, I mean I decided to submit to the will of God for my life; therefore, I was sold out to His purpose and the predestined path He has for my life. I awoke every morning in pursuit of God and his plan.

After a random fall in 2011, I began experiencing pain and discomfort in my lower back. I ignored signs for a while, hoping it would go away. Eventually, I saw a neurosurgeon and made up my mind that I wasn't having surgery. But of course, he recommended it. "But I can't have surgery!" I thought. I had just recently launched my ministry, published my first book, *and* started to work with a nonprofit that served young girls in the community.[8] I was active in my church and other affiliations related to my passion for women's ministry. Who had time for surgery?

Not me.

After months of avoiding and dealing with excruciating pain but keeping on, I had to make a decision. So, with the surgeon now relentlessly nudging, I agreed to have the surgery in November 2012. The doctor assured me that it wouldn't be too bad. I was terrified at the thought of having back surgery. I was advised it would be no more than a two-day stay in the hospital, six weeks of recovery, and then back to life I go!

---

[8] Book reference: *Practical Principles for the 3D Woman*

It didn't happen that way. The five-hour surgery was longer than initially explained. I woke up with no feeling in my left leg. I now had a form of paralysis in my leg with no sensation and severe numbness in my lower extremities. What was supposed to have been a six-week-and-two-day process turned into 11 days in the hospital, 7 days in a rehab hospital, 45 days of home therapy, and several months of outpatient therapy, doctor appointments, allergic reactions, swelling, numbness, countless painful nights, wheelchairs, walkers, a rollator, canes, lack of mobility, and learning to walk all over again.

Life took a major shift.

I began a journey of faith and belief in God at another level. I experienced major losses during this season, starting with the lack of mobility and, eventually, my job. Since I needed more time to recover and rehab, I couldn't return to work within the timeframe they expected, and my employer wasn't willing to hold my position. I felt I was losing the ability to press through this season with all the odds against me. However, I knew all along God must have had a plan to do so much more than I could ask or think according to the power working in me! I realized that destiny was still mine, and although I was limited physically, there were no limitations in my spirit. The spirit prompted me to write about my experience and process daily, as I trusted GOD for not only healing but His will to be done in my life! I eventually wrote a devotional entitled *NOT Even THIS will STOP ME: Overcoming Painful Distractions While Pursuing Destiny*!

I have come to discover that limitations start in the mind. I could have submitted to the physical limitation of my season, got stuck, stop pursuing and producing. Instead, I submitted my process to the plan of God and shifted my perspective about why I was in the season!

Let God use you where you are for His Glory! There are NO LIMITATIONS in HIM! When you are living a life submitted to Him, everything you go through is under His authority. Even your pain has a purpose. Trust your process, accept what He allows, and know that even your limitations can be liberating to bring Him the greatest GLORY!

—*Living Without Limits Because I Serve a Limitless God*

Is This unto Death?

AUNTIE,

March 16, 2019, you left us…

As far back as I can remember, you were always there, even if it was from afar. You were one of the best kinds of aunties to have; you were so loving and funny with a huge personality. You were always honest—you really told it like it was, with no holding back; I have always appreciated that about you. You had the ability to light up a room with just your smile or a wink of your eye.

I remember hearing you were in the hospital and knowing I had to come and see about you. You were still yourself, but I knew you weren't well. And even though it hurt to find out it was cancer, I still didn't understand your particular situation's magnitude or severity. I know cancer is serious, but I've seen people pull through, so I expected the same for you. I began to pray and solicited others to pray with me on your behalf. I believed that God would heal you on this side, but I never saw it happening the way it did.

I came by the hospital at least every other day to sit with you and hold your hand. You said, "I need you to help your cousins through this." I had no idea what you were asking me to do until you were gone. Even now, when I think about it, they seemed to help me more than I helped them.

It was so hard losing you, and I never understood God's plan. Selfishly, I thought of other people God could have taken, but He chose you. You knew I loved you, and I know you loved me, but I felt like we all needed more time.

I remember coming into the hospital room and you not being able to talk; I don't even know if you knew we were there. I just remember coming in and sitting in silence and disbelief at what was happening right before my eyes. I remember asking myself, "God, why are you doing this?" I remember kissing your forehead and walking out of the room for the last time. I remember the feelings of hopelessness and anger: it almost felt like my heart was being ripped from my chest while I was still alive. I will never forget that day for as long as I live.

Cancer sucks, and it took you from us, but God healed you on the other side. I am grateful for the time He gave us with you and all the precious memories that can never be taken from us. You were and will always be our special kind of Rose.

—I Thank God for Your Life

Hey Girl, Hey!

HEY GIRL, HEY!

Recently, I was depressed and unsettled in my emotions, thoughts, and actions. After deciding that I needed to explore my life in new ways, I internalized every decision I made. I decided to do something spontaneous and to take a LEAP.

This LEAP of change was something I felt I needed so I could express myself. I needed to redefine the life I had into a better, more vibrant life. I wanted to be FREE: free from others' opinions and free from social and emotional turmoil, so I set out on a quest to redesign my life into something NEW.

I never calculated the endurance of sacrifice that would take place. I had to learn myself all over again. After months of feeling inadequate and hopeless and moments of feeling faithless, I decided I needed to change some things.

One early morning, I drove. What should have taken 4 to 4.5 hours turned into a 6-hour trip. I started the drive in silence to refocus and settle my mind. During this time, I begin to reflect on each area of my life: finance, romance, faith, family, friends, education, career, self-care, mental health, etc. As I was driving, I began to have a conversation with myself:

- ★ First, I released myself and granted a voice to the emotions I had been experiencing. Understanding that my sentiment was real, I acknowledged I have power through perspective. Although I had accomplished so much in my life and within the year, I was bound by circumstances.

- Next, I began to acknowledge my life through gratitude. I made a mental list of all the good in my life. I was able to address each area of my life that was healthy, freeing, and all of the things going well.
- Then, I stopped to examine my faith and what it meant for me to have faith. I begin to pray aloud while driving, straightforward conversation with myself and my God. I remembered what has kept me during times of turmoil, what God had promised me through His word, through prophecy, and through dialogue in prayer.
- Lastly, I built myself mentally, emotionally, and spiritually by affirming my WHY in life through scripture and my own personal values.

Every day, I strive to be the best version of myself. I'm learning to articulate my feelings, my perspective, and adjust according to my health. Through embracing my journey, I've chosen to always extend honor, seek counseling, and live in peace, joy, and happiness.

—On My Way to Already Alright

Behold My Sister

BEHOLD, MY SISTER,

The time is NOW!

I can recall the ringing in my soul to pursue. All I kept hearing was, "Behold, I will do a New Thing!" I felt this overwhelming weight to press in purpose like I had never pressed. I began to tell myself, "It is time for you to forge forward as you have never forged before." I've always been taught that if I have the authority to say it, it's time for the action needed to pursue it.

It is a new season, a new day, and it's my TIME!

Many women have great ideas, aspirations, goals, objectives, desires, dreams, and wishes. It is almost second nature for us to speak of the things we desire to have, achieve, and experience. Today, expressions like "YOLO" ("You only live once") and "Bucket Lists" have become a part of our vocabulary.

Many desire the dream car, home, vacation, spouse, career, ministry, and life. However, the challenge is embracing that we deserve it, having the courage to pursue what we want, and employing the faith that will manifest it in your space.

I had to embrace it! I had to accept that it was my time. I had to accept that what I desired could be mine. I've had to accept God's choice for me and for the future He has designed for me. Regardless of my past, my background, my shortcomings, I trust there is more for me! I've accepted that what God has for me is truly for me. The possibilities are endless, but I had to accept that it was my time, and it is always my time!

I needed courage! I knew that I embodied a spirit of bravery and strength in the face of difficulty because of the many challenges I have endured. I just didn't realize I needed to ramp up my courage for the pursuit. For a moment, I was stuck right here. I knew I could have it; I embraced the concept of having it; now I have to pursue it! Wait…that takes something that requires a press! My goodness! For me to pursue anything, it will take courage. It takes courage to lose weight. It takes courage to go back to school, to enter a new relationship, to start a new ministry project, or to pursue the will and purpose of God.

Lord, don't let me get stuck in the courage phase of my journey.

I have to get to NOW! What do I need to get there? I guess I have to buckle down, be determined, and PRESS! It takes courage to go after what you want and FAITH for it to manifest.

The Bible says so much about faith:

> *"To have faith is to be sure of the things we hope for, to be certain of the things we cannot see."*
> HEBREWS 11: 1 GNT

> *"No one can please God without faith, for whoever comes to God must have faith that God exists and rewards those who seek him."*
> HEBREWS 11:6 GNT

Through His Word, I understood that to manifest my desire, I needed to employ faith.

Faith is the ability to HOPE when you have no evidence. I had to hope, act, and believe. I've learned to make my confessions, mix in a little action, add a bunch of courage, put in a pinch of faith, and TRUST the process.

It's my TIME!

No more delays. I had to accept that there was more for me. Today, I am grateful because I am embracing that I can have it: mustering up the courage to pursue and EXPECTING to see the manifestation of all my desires. My time is truly NOW. I'm walking in my New Thing!

—I Have Beheld the Great Works of the Lord

Blessings in the Storm

Thank You After All

TO MY SISTERS,

I wish you knew how hard it was to be expendable. I give you all the best of me, yet you could care less if I'm in the room. So many times, you get together, laughing and talking for hours on end, and you're so unbothered by the absence of my presence. When people ask where I am, my placement is excused away like missing keys, just lying around somewhere. I'm not just lying around. I'm distant because I don't feel welcomed. From the moment I appeared to be different from you all, you set me aside. Like loose candy in the bottom of mothers' purse, I wasn't what you wanted. People always think I'm exaggerating about the way you disregard me, but it's true.

For seven years, I've given up my dreams and taken care of our ailing mother. I've changed her, made sure she ate, slept in hospital rooms, and sent my child to stay with friends so I could live in waiting rooms and leave from there to go to work. I lost sleep, gained weight, lost hair, and gained heartache only for you all to rest well in your own lives; you lived at my expense. You had nothing to worry about because I took care of everything. I was everywhere, and any place I couldn't be, I paid for someone to be there. Anything I could not do, I paid to have done.

You wanted her to live in a nursing home because you didn't want to do the work. You got together and decided that you knew what was best for the mother I had been taking care of. You had no money to put her anywhere, so you needed a reason to get me out of the home I was in, the only home I'd ever known. You got together and decided that I had no right to make any decisions about anything happening in my home. You got together and composed legal documentation to keep me out and keep me away. I never wanted to fight you all, but you put me on the opposing side and never let me choose.

I used to cry to God and ask him to heal the wounds you all caused. I wanted my healing to be your pain. I wanted my reward to cost you what your reward cost me. I wanted God to cover my scars and deepen yours. I hoped he'd send you all back to apologize; I wanted God to cause you to lose everything you tried to take from me.

One day, when I was exhausted from being broken, God reminded me of Joseph. Joseph was Jacob's favorite. All his brothers knew he was the favorite, and they still chose to take Joseph away from his father and sell him into slavery. They thought getting rid of Joseph would make life easier for them. Instead, it hurt the one they all loved. Joseph's life took him on a journey from a pit, to slavery, to a palace, and in that palace, those same brothers came back and needed Joseph. God showed me that despite what the brothers thought they were doing, He still had Joseph covered and was going to bring Joseph out just fine.

So many times, I've wept at you leading me astray and causing me to feel like I wasn't right to be a part of you. I hated you, but I learned that the time I spent hating you was wasted. It was not getting me to the place God had for me.

Just like Joseph, God's got me.

For placing me on a path that would take me to a pit of depression, I forgive you. For selling me over to the chains of low self-esteem, I forgive you. For the time I spent in a prison of anxiety, I forgive you. For the lesson that—no matter what—God's got me, I thank you. I may have never come this way without you. I thought I would hate you forever, but I guess this is, "Thank you."

—God's Got Me

I Need You

Ladies,

You know, sometimes our esteem is not where it needs to be. And based on our life experiences, negative self-esteem can't take us to the positive places we need to go. Because of this, I am so grateful for the women in my life who have shown me what it is to truly be a woman. They have shown me—not general strength, but vulnerability and openness. They have shown me something different than independence. They are showing me their need for me, and by doing so, they show me my need for them.

It is amazing to me that we live in a world where so often women are congratulated on their independence, black women especially. In today's culture, there is a normative rhythm of needing to be self-sufficient at all costs. Self-sufficiency is good. It is indeed important, yet self-sufficiency can also be self-destructive because the reality is: I need you just as much as you need me, especially woman to woman.

Too often, we pride ourselves on the very things that separate us. Independence doesn't bring us together as much as vulnerability does, yet vulnerability is exactly what we shun because we're so hell-bent on attempting to be something that we were not created to be—alone. And we do this for the sake of what looks like success when this show of independence simply marks a pathway toward isolation, and ultimately, self-destruction.

Indeed, I am deeply grateful for the women in my life who have shown me that I could need them. I am grateful for the women in my life who have shown me that I could love them. I am grateful for the women in my life who have shown me that I could use them. By being able to love them, need them, and use them, I have found the importance of doing the same with myself.

I have found the freedom to live through being able to show up for myself in the way that my ladies have shown up for me. Though I wasn't always ready for the love that was shown or the depths that were provided, I'm so grateful for the connections that have changed my life forever. I'm looking forward to not only more of these connections for myself, but I look forward to creating a pathway for others to connect with themselves through readily connecting with me. To all of this, I say:

HELLO, MY SISTERS,

I'm here.
I hear you. I need you, and I am listening.

—I Need You, and You Need Me

Good. Girl. Friends.

Dear Sisters Who Have Gone On,

Lately, when I hear the theme song of the old television series Golden Girls, I belt out, "Thank you for being my friend." To my sisters: D, I, R, S, and L, I want to say thank you for being my good girl friends. The exact dates of when you walked on have faded, and although I don't yet think of you as ancestors, I celebrate your birthdays and your favorite holidays.

From the first of you thirty years ago to the last one a year ago, you have taught me that no matter how sudden or expected, it's always a shock to the spirit. One is never ready to lose another human being forever. The unbearable heartache first turns into warm, daily reminders, and now, waves of quick glimpses or long conversations.

D, growing up together was one big giggle fest. Your unusual laugh-until-you-snort still makes my face hurt just thinking about how good the laughter was. We were good church girls, and we grew to be women of God. We were so young, and even though time is never promised to us, I thought we would have more, like our moms would enjoy. My girls were with me to mourn you, and I pledged them to be the best friend that I could be to them.

I and R, how odd that both of you—feisty Latinas, women of great faith, colleagues, married with children—were each making the world spin. Then, bam! Terminally ill. We were sisters, and the love was truly genuine. You both taught me a deep sense of loyalty, compassion, and hugs. I, after your passing, R and I would run to a conference room and cry until our eyes hurt, and then we would say to each other, imitating your voice, "It's okay, my darlings. My angels." R, as you weakened, we learned to say these words to each other when you could no longer hug with your arms or speak: "The love was in your eyes. I hope you could see it in mine."

S, you were my first "grown lady" friend, and it was never a dull moment for this little college student on her own. You saw me and welcomed me to be your sister. God and family were everything to you, and I appreciate you living your life out loud. You were a real-life example of a confident, godly woman leader who took control of every situation in an authentic woman's way. I am still discovering your life lessons.

L, your Mother Earth, natural, Sistah Girl lifestyle and thinking was the mutual encouragement we needed to be authentically who we were created to be. You lived by "God will provide" and were stubborn to a fault. As your body failed, I thought you were giving up, but I realized it was your surrender to God's will.

Thank you for trusting God.

I want to say thank you for being my good girl friends.

—Still Pledging to Be the BEST Friend to Girls You Leave Behind

I Call You Sister

My Sister,

Most people define sisters as having the same mother or same father. For us, it was having the same heart.

As both my cousin and my sister, you have been a constant in my life for as long as I can remember. We are the true definition of the saying, "From the cradle to the grave."

You probably can't imagine why I am writing you this letter. The first reason is to thank you for always accepting me and always celebrating me when we were children. I remember one time in particular when I was asked about the scars on my body. You got so upset and told that person off. You said, "Don't ask her that," and "Don't worry about how she got them." In those moments, I felt protected by you. You, standing up for me, helped me build my confidence as we got older.

I'm sure you remember the hair struggles I had. You had the long, beautiful hair from grandma's side of the family. Let's just say that I must have gotten the hair gene from my dad. I didn't feel pretty next to you for a very long time. As I got older, I realized that had nothing to do with you; it was my insecurities that made me uncomfortable, so I thank you for being a voice for me before I found my own. The love you had and have, for me, has built a bond that can never be broken. It forces us to make sure our own children are close like we were.

I won't say things have always been perfect between us, but I can say that whenever we need each other, we are going to show up. During the times I felt alone, I always knew you were there. There was never a time I called you when you weren't happy to hear my voice.

You will never know how much it meant to me when you came to see me in Hawaii. To be far away from family is very hard. At that point in my life, I needed family more than anybody could imagine. I went through so many things while living out of the country, and most times, there was no family in sight. Thank you for being a breath of sunshine and fresh air in a time when I needed it the most.

The one thing I value the most is your kind heart and loving spirit. You have endured some rough times as we have matured in our lives. Your endurance and will to succeed is beyond compare. I honor your hard work and dedication to your daughters.

So, what do I call you?

Our mothers are sisters, so that makes us cousins, but more than that, I call you my sister because life has shaped us to love each other in that way.

I love you.

Keep pushing.

You are worthy.

—Your Sister

Control

Dear Sisters Who Need to Be in Control,

I used to pride myself on my ability to control any situation. At the top of my game, I could maintain control and make it look effortless. The accolades gave me confirmation that I was good at it.

I could even juggle situations confidently and calmly on the outside. I felt like a pair of control top pantyhose! I had all the moving parts restrained. Every detail of the situation that could be seen was taut, smooth, sheer, and transparent. No sagging, no bagging. Everything was well put together. I even began to believe I was in control of being in control. I never paid much attention to how things looked or felt on the inside.

Most would find it odd to think about control top pantyhose if you heard your executive director announce an immediate staff reduction. I had been through staff reductions before, and my first thought was always: I've never been unemployed; I'm a control top woman, and my work in this setting is not complete. For a moment, I thought about the manufacturer and inspector of the control top. Previously, I hadn't really considered all the others and their hopes in this situation. There was a flaw in my thinking. The control was gone, and I certainly wasn't on top. This announcement was like a defective pair of control-top pantyhose. Busted—and with no control. Take it from me: when you're struggling alone, and your pantyhose stop short of your waist, you are not covered. There is nothing YOU can do in any situation until you realize you are just like this busted pair of "control tops."

I remember the scene like it were yesterday…

It was a grueling week of being stunned, numb, feeling anger, and deep despair while waiting for the other shoe to drop. I couldn't eat nor sleep. This feeling of being out of control was so unfamiliar. I couldn't get my bearings. My thoughts were all over the place. Everything I knew about being in control—planning for everything, mapping each action from start to finish didn't come. I needed to be in control even though I couldn't focus. I was depressed and desperate. It was no longer about being without a job. This was the point where I surrendered the thought of being a control top girl because finally, I realized I was never ever in control of being in control.

When I could no longer look to myself to assure the desired outcome, I felt a calmness that was unfamiliar. I didn't hear God speak. Although my mind continued to recount to God why I needed my job, my heart was thankful and light as I stepped out of the busted pantyhose that gave me no real control or security. When I opened my heart to follow whoever God places in control, my confidence returned.

So, sisters, I'm leaving the club. I don't need to be in control, and I'm grateful. I hope you will join me because God is able!

—Relinquishing Control Because God is in Control

It's Almost Time

To the Woman Who's Been Waiting:

I understand all too well where you are. You have dreams that you've been afraid to start. You've been waiting on the right moment, and every time you're almost there—every time you have the nerve—things happen that shake you. I have been you. Sometimes, I'm still you.

As a little girl, I had dreams of being a dancer. I watched the greats and eventually wanted to be a dance teacher. I could see it as clear as day when I laid down. My dreams were ambitious, but as a child, I had no fear. We aren't born with fear; we learn it.

Even though I had big dreams for myself, so did everyone else. Some people wanted me to be a nurse. Some people wanted me to be a teacher. Everybody had an idea for who they wanted me to be, and when I told them what I wanted, they told me it was unrealistic. How many times can you be told that you won't be something before you take it to heart? To make everyone happy, I tried to fit into so many of their roles for me that I wore myself down. While I was so busy chasing the dreams that others had for me, I let my dreams fall by the wayside.

By the time the dreams I had in the depths of my heart resurfaced back to memory, they felt like they were on the other side of the world. An anxious mind found every reason not to go after my dreams. A busy life kept me away from chasing them. Lack of support allowed me to doubt myself. I prayed. I cried. And I asked God to show me just one more time if the dreams I saw so vividly for myself were the plans He had for me.

One day, I stumbled upon Proverbs 16:3 on social media for the first time: "Commit to the Lord whatever you do, and He will establish your plans." I had never read it before, and it was exactly what I needed. I kept that scripture in my heart, but I was still afraid.

God was showing me that it was a part of His plan for me, but I just didn't see how it would happen. I guess I was kind of like Sarai. God told me what He would do, but because He hadn't done it when I expected Him to, I was looking for ways to solve the situation myself. I was looking for Ishmael when God had promised me Isaac.

I tried so many ways to make it happen. I wanted my dreams to come true! I forced myself into places that I thought would give me what I needed to turn my dreams into reality. I got close so many times. I didn't know it then, but even though I knew where I was trying to go, I just wasn't ready to be there.

I had some lessons I needed to learn before God could just let me have it. I had to learn to compromise. I needed to give out some forgiveness. I had to learn to trust and be less reactive. I had to learn to hold my tongue. Not to mention, there were relationships out there that I had to let go of and some that I needed to build. Until I went through some things that gave me those lessons, I wouldn't be able to properly handle where God would allow me to go. Without these lessons, I would have missed reaching my full potential because I would have mishandled too many things along the way.

Time went by, and I kept my dreams in my heart, but I kept living and learning as well. I actually began to invest in small things I would need when the time came. I stepped out on faith in a couple of areas where I felt more confident. I kept praying, and I kept going. Then, all of a sudden, a woman I least expected brought me an idea that would move my dreams to reality.

We had never talked about my plans before, and I honestly never saw a reason to. This woman brought me the missing piece I needed. My bond with her was one of those relationships I needed to build. Her plan just needed my skill. It was a kairos moment.[9] I'm still praying for the perfect time to move, but now I know God never forgot about me.

---

[9] kai·ros : / ˈkīräs/ : noun meaning right, critical or crucial (moment)

You see, God is rewarding my patience just like He will reward yours. I know you've been waiting, and sometimes it feels like what you're waiting for will never come. Keep going, Sis. Keep giving your all. Because when the time comes that your dreams and reality collide, you will know it was worth every moment that you waited.

It's Almost Time!

—I'm Praying for You

Role Models

DEAR STRONG WOMEN,

The older I get, and the more I learn about me, the more I know I was blessed early in life. Long before I ever knew what 'role model' meant, many of you were already shaping me profoundly. I am grateful for being surrounded by you and how you 'see' me. You are interested in what I have to say and what I am thinking. I am important to you even on those occasions when it is clear I had nothing to offer you. The first time I met each of you, I found you fascinating; it's been humbling to discover the feeling is mutual.

I feel loved and safe with you. However, the world paints a much different picture of strong women—pristine, privileged, ageless, slim, white, blonde women in business suits and pumps. They are self-made, never in the presence of other women, and always serious. This version of the strong woman never looks truly happy, yet she's always smiling.

Mama, long before I was able to reconcile the two worlds we were born into, you; my grandmas; aunties; kindergarten, second-, and fourth-grade teachers; and my Sunday School teacher with her Angela Davis afro and giant hoop earrings—all of whom are gone now—were already protecting my soil, planting seeds, and tending my growth to becoming one of you.

I remember like it was yesterday—not so much the details anymore beyond my favorite white dress with embroidered butterflies with buttons at the tips of their antennas—how I felt when I was three or four years old. I would spend time with my two college girl playmates. I felt like a big girl when I was with them. They engaged me in conversation and introduced me to their friends. They asked for my opinion before making decisions about what we would eat or do next. My strong women's circle was widening even then.

I depend daily on my strong woman guide created by all of you and those yet to come. I have been divinely favored and blessed with a lifetime of strong women. I recognize that I continue to morph into more of me each time I am with each of you or when I think about the worn hands and aprons of my grandmas. I have come to rely on your soft-spoken hopes and practical lessons. It amazes me to think that most of you would never meet one another, nor were you all known to me at one time.

I know for sure that I am a strong woman of faith because of you and my grandmas—all of you, strong women of God. I just wished they could see the results of their prayers and planting. I try my best to share the seeds you planted in me by planting seeds in the soil of women and girls, and I find myself honored to know these young women because every woman deserves an image of a strong woman crafted just for her.

AGAIN,
I want to thank you.

—I am Forever Grateful

contributors

Lady **PAULA COTTON** is a mentor, facilitator, author, pastoral counselor, and leadership coach. She obtained certification in Missional Involvement through New Orleans Baptist Theological Seminary. Lady Paula enjoys shopping, writing, praying, and connecting with the love of her life, Pastor J Scott Cotton.

Dr. **LATISHA REEVES HENRY** is a wife, mother, a dynamic preacher, speaker, teacher, author, and coach. She inspires others with a powerful message of hope and biblical strategies to dare them to be the best God created them to be.

KAMARA OWENS is a native of Jacksonville, Florida. As a mother, mentor, and active blogger, Kamara pours into teens and young adults, encouraging them not to limit themselves to what others expect. Kamara inspires others to be all God has called them to be.

REGINA ROBERTS is a professional Christian life coach and higher education professional. She serves as a Christian coach in ministry for millennials and women, where she educates, enriches, and empowers women. Regina enjoys traveling, reading, and spending quality time with family and friends.

MONIQUE ROSS is a widow and mother of three beautiful daughters. She has traveled the world and experienced life outside of the usual comforts. Monique hails from a large family, which gives her insight and wisdom to objectively approach ever-changing personalities and the trials that come with growth.

VALORA K STARR is committed to serving God's people, especially women and girls as they discover their spiritual gifts. She is an advocate for justice and building the beloved community. Auntie Val loves passing on family stories and spending time in conversation with four-year-olds.

TARYN "LOVEREIGNS" WHARWOOD is a mentor, host, curator, advocate, educator, entrepreneur, and much more. Love is Co-Founder of The Cypher Open Mic Poetry & Soul, founder of Artis(Tree) Live and The Artis(Tree) Youth Project, founder of The Closet Jax, and Owner/CEO of I AmLoveReigns Enterprises LLC.

CHANTELL WILLIAMS was born and raised in Jacksonville, Florida to Victor and Phyllis Bradley. As the owner of The Total Woman Consulting Agency, Chantell extends this community leadership to her church. She serves as a young adult leader among other roles within the ministry.

COACH D NICOLE is a charming and spirited first-class coach passionate about encouraging, supporting, and coaching others through personal and business endeavors. As a transformational life coach and pastor, she is most loved for her wit, boisterous personality, and direct and upfront coaching style.

www.ingramcontent.com/pod-product-compliance
Lightning Source LLC
Chambersburg PA
CBHW030324100526
44592CB00010B/556

LETTERS TO MY SISTERS
Pain, Poise, Pride, and God's Promise

Too often, women pass one another by as if living different lives in different spaces. However, wisdom teaches that women largely live the same lives in different bodies. Together, women live through insecurity, depression, being overlooked and being misunderstood. Whether women share identical experiences, the goal of being loved, included, and supported is common among many. No matter if they are rich or poor, black or white, African or Asian, womanly connection transcends demographics. By appreciating this value, women can finally behold the beauty of sharing sisterhood beyond racial, generational, and geographical bounds.

With **LETTERS TO MY SISTERS**: *Pain, Poise, Pride, and God's Promise*, ten women share letters from their hearts to expose intimate life details that all women will relate to in some way. As women engage this book, the hope is that the sharing of these letters provides a gateway for other women to share in like manner.

No longer should women keep their herstory private. As women increasingly share, they rewrite the tragic history of silence. With these letters, women commit to saying what they mean to say and healing in formally forbidden areas of life. This book was written to encourage sisters all over the world to share and release stories of their own.

LETTERS TO MY SISTERS was written from the heart. The writings will prick women's hearts and draw women to each other as women draw closer to theirselves.

Women / Self-Help / Self-Management

ISBN 978-1-942650-46-1

On the Worship of God

Vintage Puritan

John Owen

GLH Publishing